Quilt
Sashings & Settings

The basics & beyond

by Jean Ann Wright

Landauer Publishing, LLC

Quilt Sashings & Settings

The basics & beyond

by Jean Ann Wright

Copyright © 2012 by Landauer Publishing, LLC
Projects Copyright © 2012 by Jean Ann Wright

This book was designed, produced, and published by Landauer Publishing, LLC
3100 101st Street, Urbandale, IA 50322
515-287-2144; 800-557-2144; www.landauercorp.com

President/Publisher: Jeramy Lanigan Landauer
Vice President of Sales & Administration: Kitty Jacobson
Editor: Jeri Simon
Art Director: Laurel Albright
Photography: Sue Voegtlin

Library of Congress Control Number: 2011943405
ISBN 13: 978-1-935726-16-6
ISBN 10: 1-935726-16-1

This book is printed on acid-free paper.
Printed in China by C & C Offset Printing Co., Ltd.
10 9 8 7 6 5 4 3 2 1

contents

introduction

My first quilt was made with four-inch-wide sashings, which was completely against my instructor's rules.

I have always been a bit of a rebel, showing just enough free spirit to slightly annoy my parents and teachers. So, it should come as no surprise that when I took my first quilting class, I didn't quite follow the instructor's rules about sashings.

She told us sashing should only be 25 - 33 percent of the finished block size and should always be cut from plain muslin. Since we were making 12" blocks, our sashings were to only be two or three-inches wide. Naturally, I chose a large print fabric and cut my sashings a daring four-inches wide. The result was a shock to the teacher and class, but I was delighted with the look my bold sashings gave the finished quilt.

My secret for creating original quilt settings—*Simplicity always works*. Your sashing or setting plan doesn't have to be complicated to produce a stunning quilt. Manipulating color, value and the scale of the fabric pattern goes a long way to adding the "wow" factor to even the most basic quilt block.

The two most common ways to sew quilt blocks together in a setting arrangement are block to block or blocks with sashings. Other setting variations include strip quilts, medallion quilts and the new setting arrangement, circle of nine. There are many more you can create.

Consider this book a journey. Sew through it and discover what you can do to make easy, fun and interesting quilts. A multitude of projects in different sizes are included for a variety of quilting experiences.

Quilting is really just play for adults. It is relaxing and brings out the creativity hidden inside each one of us. By having your own small rebellion and making an unexpected design change you can end up with a finished quilt that is an expression of individuality.

about the author

I have been sewing and making quilts since I was in pre-school. I learned very early that I am a tactile person and I simply love the feel of fabric in my hand. After studying textiles and fine arts at Palm Beach State College I combined these two interests to become a fiber artist. I am sure my mother never envisioned me spending a lifetime and career sewing one piece of fabric to another when she gave me two pieces of fabric to play with so she could finish making a sundress for me to wear.

From 1986 to 2007 I was editor-in-chief of the international quilting magazine, QUILT, along with a variety of special interest quilting titles with the same publishing company. Since retiring from full time editing I have worked as a consultant in the quilting industry designing quilts for major fabric manufacturers and popular quilting magazines. I have recently designed a vintage fabric collection, Charleston 1850, for Newcastle Fabrics.

A love of travel led me to teach quilt workshops in all regions of the United States, including the prestigious Houston Quilt Festival, and also in Canada and England. When I teach I try to encourage my students to avoid the safe choices and instead see what new images they can create when they step out of their comfort zone.

When I first started quilting with purpose, I worked hard to perfect my skills to enter judged and juried shows. After winning a number of awards, including an award for best original design at the IQA in Houston, Texas (many years ago), and the best of show for folk art in Boca Raton, Florida, I decided it was more fun to simply sew quilts whether they were award winners or not. I relaxed and started to design and sew quilts just for the fun of it.

In playing with quilt design I discovered that a small change could turn a simple quilt setting into an interesting and clever quilt design. It was a relief to know I didn't have to sew a block with 50 little pieces or make an elaborate setting scheme to end up with a uniquely designed quilt. Simply by manipulating the color and fabric choices, a quilt with a basic block design and easy sashings and settings can become an original creation much admired by everyone.

My first book, **Circle of Nine**, was co-authored with my sister Janet Houts. Quilting together has brought us closer. In **Circle of Nine** we introduce a new quilt setting that is enjoying popularity with quilters who want to keep their sewing simple yet make a quilt that is not like any other. Two circle of nine quilts are included in this book of sashings and settings, one designed by Janet and one by myself.

I am thrilled to share all of the little "tricks" I have learned over the years to make a unique quilt using simple techniques. Try making some of the projects in this book, then feel free to branch out and mix and match the settings to express your own creativity.

Jean Ann Wright

Choosing Fabric and Color

Color, value and scale are the three main things to consider when choosing fabrics.

Sounds easy, doesn't it? Only three things to remember as you pluck fabrics off the shelf in your favorite quilt shop. Unfortunately, it's a little more challenging than a shopping trip and there are a few things to consider when collecting fabrics for a quilt.

Most quilters find choosing fabric colors the most challenging and rewarding part of quilt making. Learning about color is not as difficult as it might seem.

A few key words and their definitions:

- Hue: a color in its purest form

- Tint: adding white to the pure hue

- Tone: adding a color's complement to the pure hue

- Shade: adding black to the pure hue

The Color Wheel

The color wheel is a popular tool designed to organize colors.

It shows us how to use colors together effectively. The color wheel has several layers rotating around the center to show various color combinations. Each color on the color wheel is the head of an entire color family. Quilt shops and hobby stores sell purse-sized color wheels, which are a very handy tool to have when shopping for fabrics.

The primary colors are red, yellow and blue. From these colors, every other color is created. The primary colors form an equilateral triangle on the color wheel and the colors between the primaries are the result of two adjacent colors being combined and creating the secondary colors of orange, green and purple. Primary and secondary colors are mixed together to create tertiary colors in red-orange, yellow-orange, yellow-green, blue-green, blue-purple and red-purple. The colors can be divided again and again to create a limitless palette of color.

Color harmony should also be considered when choosing colors for your project. Harmony in color is the same as harmony in music, all the individual elements combine to create a pleasing whole.

- Analogous:
  a harmony of adjacents: a color scheme using colors adjacent to each other on the color wheel.

- Complementary:
  a harmony of opposites: a color scheme using colors that are opposite each other on the color wheel.

- Split Complementary:
  a featured single color and the two colors on each side of its complementary color.

- Triadic:
  any three colors that form an equilateral triangle on the color wheel.

- Tetradic:
  any four colors that form a square on the color wheel.

- Monochromatic:
  variations of a single color, this can include tints, shades and tones of the chosen color.

The color possibilities keep growing by adding white, black, or a complementary color. The colors will continue to change as you use the hue, tint, tone and shade of each color.

A Helping Hand
Don't spend hours agonizing over which colors to use in your quilt. It's easy to let someone else do it for you. Advertising agencies put maximum time and effort into selecting the most effective colors for their ads. Tear out ads that capture your attention and file them away for future reference. When you are unsure what colors to choose for a new quilt, pull out an ad or photo to use as a guide in selecting fabrics.

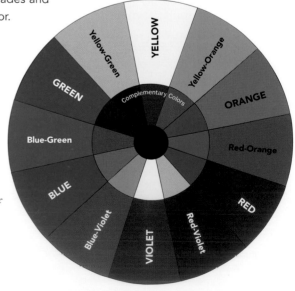

Seasonal Colors
The simplified method

A less scholarly approach to choosing colors for a quilt project is the simplified method of classifying colors into families with the names of the seasons. If you are unsure of a color palette for your next quilt, simply make one to match the seasonal weather that is taking place right outside your sewing room window.

- Tint: Spring is the season when bits of color pop out on the trees and up from the ground. These lovely pastels are created by adding white to the hues.

- Hue: Summer is the hottest season of the year with the sun shining brightly. This is the season for pure, bright colors.

- Tone: Autumn is a bit more complex. The colors can be intense, but toned down a bit. Use a bit of a color's complement for a rich full-bodied hue.

- Shade: Winter is a gray season with clouds laden with snow. Add just a touch of black to the colors to make a shade of the original.

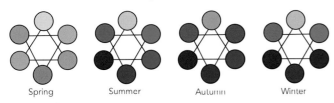

Spring   Summer   Autumn   Winter

Value
Value in relationship to color refers to how light or dark a color appears.

Artists often work with a value scale made up of approximately 10 shades of gray, starting with white and ending with black, to help them determine the value of a color. You can use a gray scale value chart against any fabric to determine how light or dark it is. Position the value scale on your fabric and find the gray value that is closest to the darkness or lightness of the main colors in your fabric.

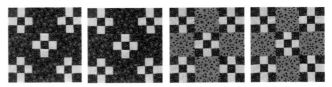

Using the value scale alone can sometimes be misleading. A fabric's value can shift to lighter or darker depending on the value of the fabric placed next to it. Sewing a sample block before you sew all of the blocks for an entire quilt can help you sort through your value choices.

Scale
The large and small of it

When quilters talk about scale, they are talking about how large or small the print is on their fabrics. Just like mixing color and value, a mix of small, medium and large scale prints adds interest to a finished quilt.

My own preference in selecting fabrics is to choose my focus fabric first, because it will almost always be a large scale, multi-color print. I usually pick a floral because I love to garden and they are among the most popular fabric patterns. I then use my focus fabric as a guide to selecting the companion fabrics I will need to make the quilt.

Look at the fabrics I have chosen to illustrate the variety of print scale available for quilting. They range from mini-prints to small prints, medium scale prints, large prints, and maxi-prints. All of these prints can be mixed into one quilt successfully. As in choosing color and value, audition your fabrics by sewing a sample block. Generally it is better

to use the largest scale prints in the biggest quilt patches and the smaller scale prints in the small patches. However, cutting a large scale print into small pieces can produce some interesting effects. Take time to play with your fabrics and be open to using them in new ways when sewing your next quilt.

Mastering the Basics

Mastering the basic units in this chapter will give you a head start on many of your quilting projects. You will discover these basic units in many quilt blocks, sashings and borders. For example, half-square triangles are used to create a variety of blocks including Churn Dash, Pinwheel and Shoo Fly. Flying Geese units provide movement in a quilt's border or sashing.

When I start a new quilt I am always excited to see how my choice of fabrics, pattern and block units will come together in the finished design. For me, seeing the finished quilt is as enjoyable as the process of sewing it together. I'm sure you will experience the same excitement as you add your unique style to the projects in this book.

You can use any of the basic units taught here in the sashings and settings of the projects in this book. Feel free to mix it up to create your own one of a kind quilt.

Quilting Shortcut Tips

- Spray starch your cut fabric pieces before marking and sewing. This gives the pieces body and holds them in place for marking lines and stitching.

- Use a ruler with non-slip dots on the back to hold it firmly in place while marking or cutting.

- Use a #2 pencil with a sharp point to make as fine a line as possible.

- Press seams each step of the way when sewing. Carefully follow any instructions given regarding which direction to press the seams.

Half-square Triangles

A half-square triangle is a basic unit commonly used in blocks or sashings. The units are stitched from two squares in different colors. The squares are cut to make pairs of half-square triangles.

Method

1 Cut (1) light fabric square and (1) dark fabric square.

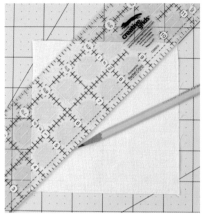

2 Draw a diagonal line from corner to corner on the wrong side of the light fabric square.

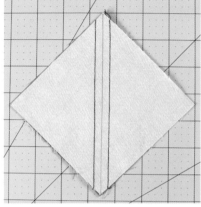

3 Lay the light fabric square on the dark fabric square, right sides together. Stitch 1/4" on either side of the drawn line.

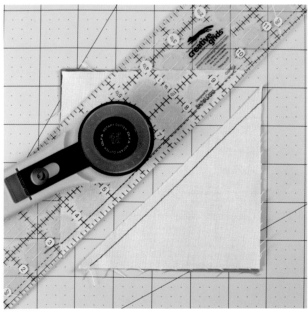

4 Cut the squares apart on the drawn line.

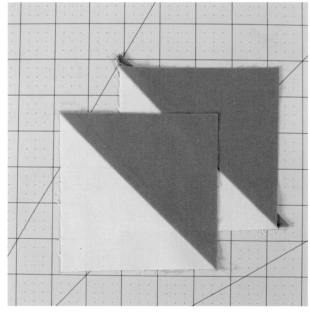

5 Press the squares open to make (2) half-square triangles. Trim the seam allowance "tails" to square up the half-square triangles. *Refer to the chart on page 13 for half-square triangle size options.*

9

Quarter-square Triangles

A quarter-square triangle is a basic unit that is also referred to as an Hourglass block. It can be used in sashing or as blocks in a quilt setting. Quarter-square triangles can be stitched in combinations of two, three or four fabrics. The method used to make the units is the same regardless of the number of fabrics in the unit.

Method (3 colors)

1 Cut (2) light fabric squares, (1) dark fabric square and (1) medium fabric square.

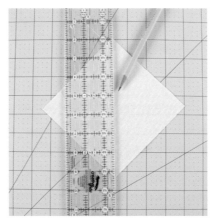

2 Draw a diagonal line from corner to corner on the wrong side of the (2) light fabric squares.

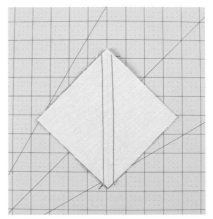

3 Lay a light fabric square on a medium fabric square, right sides together. Stitch 1/4" on either side of the drawn line. Repeat with the remaining light and dark fabric squares.

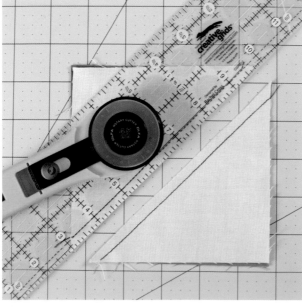

4 Cut the squares apart on the drawn line.

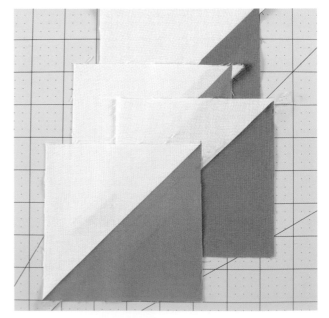

5 Press the seams toward the darker triangles to make (4) half-square triangle units, (2) in each color combination. Trim the seam allowance "tails" to square up the half-square triangle units.

Method (3 colors) *continued*

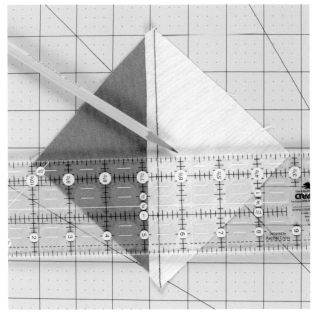

6 Draw a diagonal line from corner to corner on the wrong side of the light/medium half-square triangle units, crossing the seam line.

7 Lay a light/medium half-square triangle on a light/dark half-square triangle, right sides together. Position the light triangles on the dark and medium triangles when you stack the two sets of triangles. Pin at the seam line to hold the half-square triangles in place as you stitch. Stitch 1/4" on either side of the drawn line.

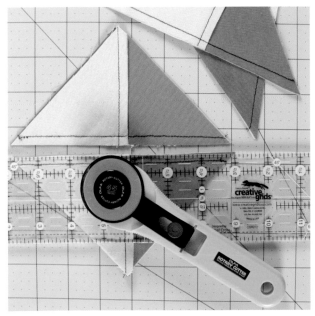

8 Cut the units apart on the drawn line.

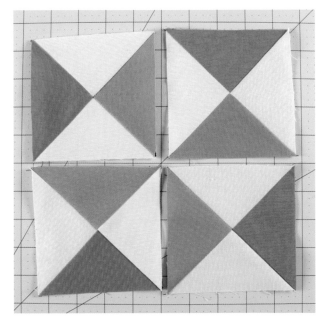

9 Press the units open to make (4) quarter-square triangles. Trim the seam allowance "tails" to square up the quarter-square triangles.
Refer to the chart on page 13 for quarter-square triangle size options.

Flying Geese

The Flying Geese unit is one of the most versatile blocks in a quiltmaker's repertoire. It is used in blocks, borders and sashings. Flying Geese units are often pieced together in rows and used in strippy quilts. They are easy to sew and give a sense of movement whenever they are used in a quilt.

Method

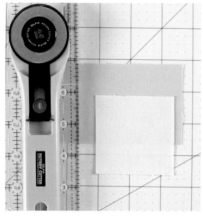

1 Cut (1) medium fabric rectangle and (2) light fabric squares.

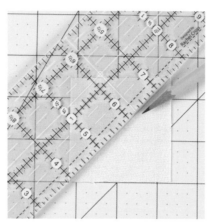

2 Draw a diagonal line from corner to corner on the wrong side of the light fabric squares.

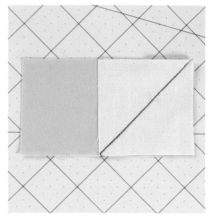

3 Lay a light fabric square on one end of the medium fabric rectangle, right sides together. Stitch on the drawn line.

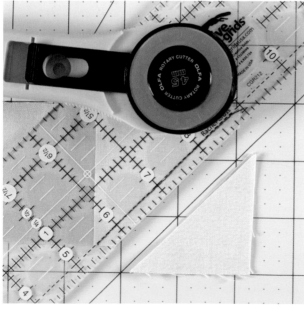

4 Trim 1/4" from the sewn line and press the seams toward the triangle.

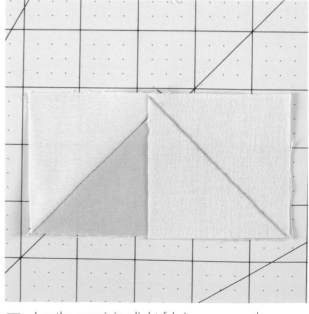

5 Lay the remaining light fabric square on the opposite end of the medium rectangle. Sew on the drawn line.

Method *continued*

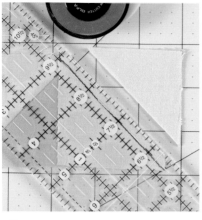

6 Trim 1/4" from the sewn line.

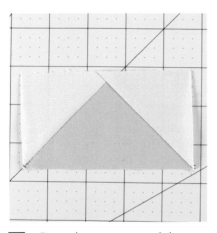

7 Press the seam toward the triangle to make a Flying Geese unit. Trim any seam allowance "tails".

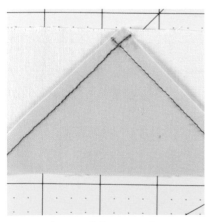

Note: The stitch lines on the wrong side of the Flying Geese unit will cross 1/4" from the "point".

Sizing Charts

*wof indicates width of fabric

Half-square Triangles

Add 7/8" to finished size of Half-square Triangle units

Finished size	Cut size	From 1 *wof strip you can get:
2"	2-7/8" squares	14
3"	3-7/8" squares	10
4"	4-7/8" squares	8
5"	5-7/8" squares	7
6"	6-7/8" squares	6

See page 9 for instructions on constructing half-square triangles.

Quarter-square Triangles

Add 1-1/4" to finished size of Quarter-square Triangle units

Finished size	Cut size	From 1 *wof strip you can get:
3"	4-1/4" squares	9
4"	5-1/4" squares	8
5"	6-1/4" squares	6
6"	7-1/4" squares	6

See page 11 for instructions on constructing quarter-square triangles.

Flying Geese

Finished size	Cut size	From 1 *wof strip you can get:
2" x 4"	2-1/2" x 4-1/2" rectangles	9
	2-1/2" squares	16
2-1/2" x 5"	3" x 5-1/2" rectangles	7
	3" squares	14
3" x 6"	3-1/2" x 6-1/2" rectangles	6
	3-1/2" squares	12

Square-in-a-Square

The Square-in-a-Square unit shares the spotlight with the Flying Geese unit as one of the most versatile. These units can be used in blocks, borders and sashings. A few simple steps and a collection of them can be sewn in a jiffy.

Method

1 Cut (1) large, medium fabric square and (4) small light fabric squares.

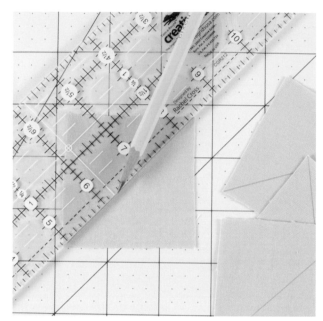

2 Draw a diagonal line from corner to corner on the wrong side of the light fabric squares.

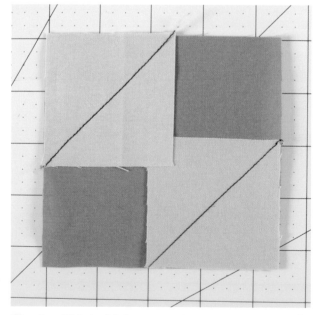

3 Lay (2) light fabric squares in opposite corners of the medium fabric square, right sides together. Sew on the drawn lines.

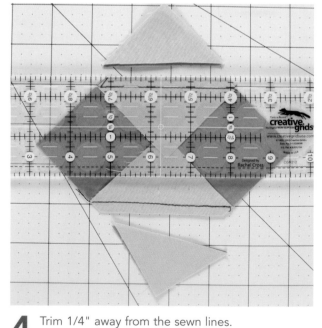

4 Trim 1/4" away from the sewn lines.

Method *continued*

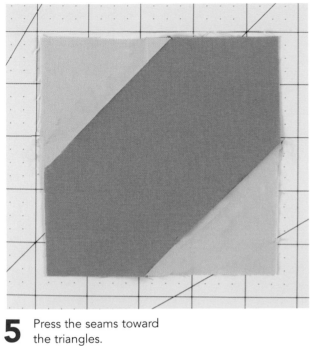

5 Press the seams toward the triangles.

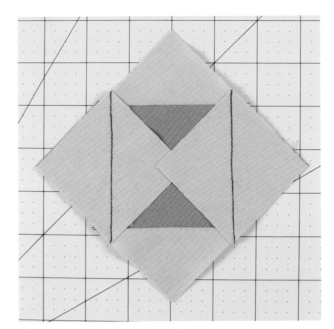

6 Lay the remaining light fabric squares in the remaining corners of the medium fabric square, right sides together. Sew on the drawn lines.

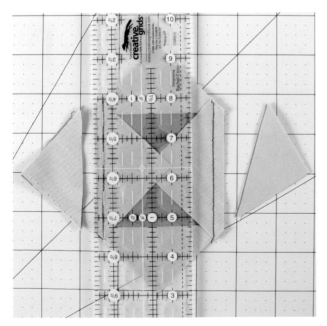

7 Trim 1/4" away from the sewn lines.

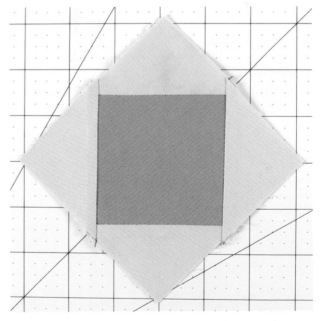

8 Press the seams toward the triangles to make a Square-in-a-Square unit. Trim any seam allowance "tails".

Refer to the chart on page 17 for Square-in-a-Square size options.

Peaks

The Peaks unit can be looked at as half of a Square-in-a-Square block or an elongated Flying Geese unit. It is most often used in combination with other units to make a finished block design.

Method

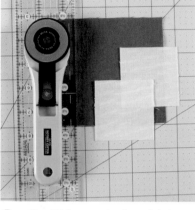

1 Cut (1) large, medium fabric square and (2) small light fabric squares.

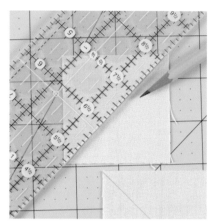

2 Draw a diagonal line from corner to corner on the wrong side of the light fabric squares.

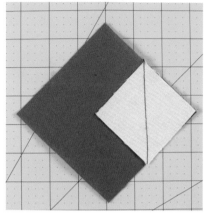

3 Lay a light fabric square in one corner of the medium fabric square. Stitch on the drawn line.

4 Trim 1/4" away from the sewn line.

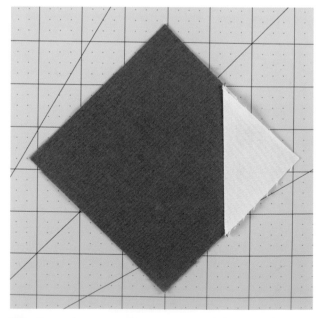

5 Press the seam allowance toward the triangle.

Method *continued*

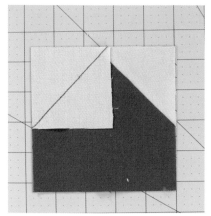

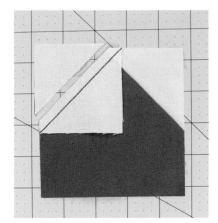

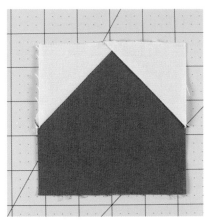

6 Lay the remaining light fabric square on the adjacent side of the medium fabric square. Stitch on the drawn line.

7 Trim 1/4" away from the sewn line.

8 Press the seam allowance toward the triangle to make a Peaks unit. Trim any seam allowance "tails".

Sizing Charts

*wof indicates width of fabric

Peaks

Finished size	Cut size	From 1 *wof strip you can get:
3"	3-1/2" squares	12
	2" squares	20
4"	4-1/2" squares	9
	2-1/2" squares	16
5"	5-1/2" squares	7
	3" squares	14
6"	6-1/2" squares	6
	3-1/2" squares	12
8"	8-1/2" squares	4
	4-1/2" squares	9

Square-in-a-Square

Finished size	Cut size	From 1 *wof strip you can get:
3"	3-1/2" squares	12
	2" squares	20
4"	4-1/2" squares	9
	2-1/2" squares	16
5"	5-1/2" squares	7
	3" squares	14
6"	6-1/2" squares	6
	3-1/2" squares	12
8"	8-1/2" squares	4
	4-1/2" squares	9

See page 14 for instructions on constructing Square-in-a-Square blocks.

Four Patch

You will find yourself using Four Patch units over and over again. A quilt can be made entirely of Four Patch units or the units can be combined with others to create different blocks. Four Patch units make interesting sashings and borders.

Method

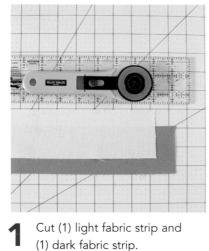

1 Cut (1) light fabric strip and (1) dark fabric strip.

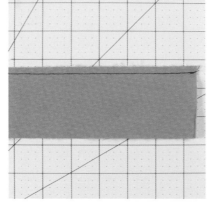

2 Lay the light and dark fabric strips, right sides together, and sew along the long edge.

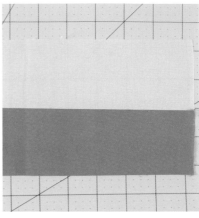

3 Press the seams toward the darker fabric strip to make a strip set.

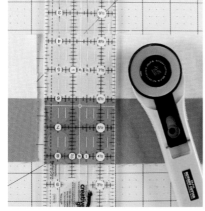

4 Cut the strip set into segments that are equal to the width of the original fabric strips.

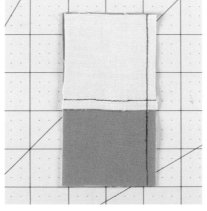

5 Lay (2) of the segments, right sides together, with the light fabric squares on the dark fabric squares. Sew along a long edge.

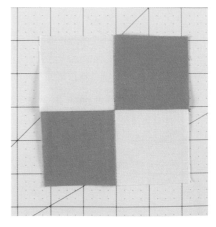

6 Press open to make a Four Patch unit.

Four Patch	*wof indicates width of fabric	
Finished size	Cut size	From 1 *wof strip you can get:
2"	2-1/2" squares	cut 16
3"	3-1/2" squares	cut 12
4"	4-1/2" squares	cut 9

Nine Patch Block

The Nine Patch block looks basic but can also be used to create complex quilt designs. Use it alone or in combination with other blocks.

Method

1 Cut (3) light fabric strips and (3) dark fabric strips.

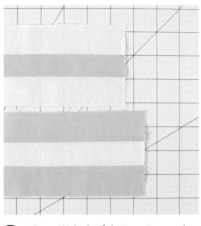

2 Sew (2) light fabric strips and (1) dark fabric strip together with the dark strip in the center to make a light/dark strip set. Sew (2) dark fabric strips and (1) light fabric strip together with the light fabric strip in the center to make a dark/light strip set. Press all seams in the strip sets toward the dark fabric.

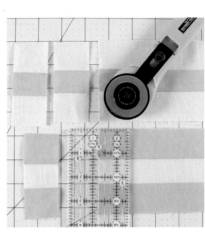

3 Cut the strip sets into segments that are equal to the width of the original fabric strips.

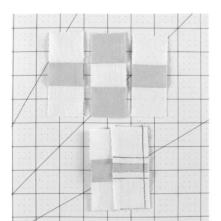

4 Lay out (2) light/dark/light segments and (1) dark/light/dark segment in rows to create a checkerboard pattern. Sew the segments together, butting the seams up against each other as you position the segments for stitching.

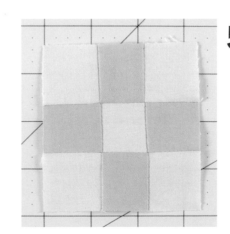

5 Press the seams away from the dark/light/dark segment to make a Nine Patch block.

Nine Patch	*wof indicates width of fabric	
Finished size	**Cut size**	**From 1 *wof strip you can get:**
1"	1-1/2" squares	28
2"	2-1/2" squares	16
3"	3-1/2" squares	12

19

Thrift Block

The Thrift block takes the Square-in-a-Square block one step further. In this block it is necessary to cut the half-square triangles and quarter-square triangles before sewing any units together. The center square of the Thrift block is often fussy cut to highlight a particular fabric motif.

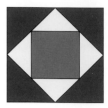

Method

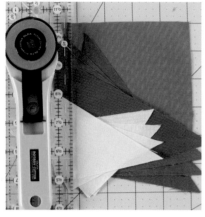

1 Cut (1) medium fabric center square 1/2" larger than the finished size. Cut (1) light fabric square 1-1/4" larger than the finished size of the center square; cut this square in half on the diagonal twice to make (4) quarter-square triangles. Cut (2) dark fabric squares 7/8" larger than the finished size of the center square; cut these squares in half on the diagonal once to make (4) half-square triangles.

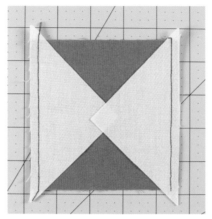

2 Lay a light fabric quarter-square triangle on opposite sides of the center square, right sides together. The tips of the triangles will overlap the center square. Sew the quarter-square triangles to the center square. Trim the "tails" and press the seams toward the quarter-square triangles.

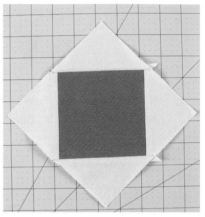

3 Lay the remaining light fabric quarter-square triangles on the remaining sides of the center square, right sides together. Sew in place and press open. Trim the "tails" to complete the center section of the block.

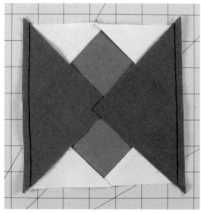

4 Lay a dark fabric half-square triangle on opposite sides of the center section of the block. Sew in place.

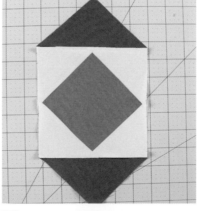

5 Trim the "tails" and press the seams toward the half-square triangles.

Refer to the chart on page 22 for Thrift block size options.

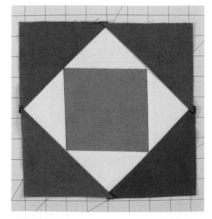

6 Lay the remaining dark fabric half-square triangles on the remaining sides of the center square, right sides together. Sew in place and press the seams toward the triangles. Trim the "tails" to complete the Thrift block.

Album X Block

This block looks challenging, but when broken down into steps it is quick and easy to sew. Use it in a garden maze setting or as a stand alone block in a modern quilt design. Traditional quilters often used muslin for the center square and signed their names or wrote a short sentiment before giving the block to a special person.

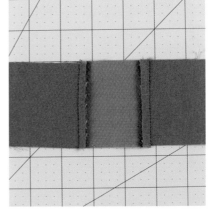

Method

1 Cut (1) medium fabric center square, (4) dark fabric rectangles and (1) light fabric square. Cut the light fabric square twice on the diagonal to make (4) quarter-square triangles.

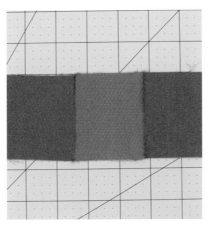

2 Sew a dark fabric rectangle to opposite sides of the medium fabric center square.

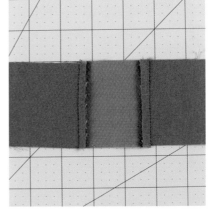

3 Press the seams toward the center square to make the block center strip.

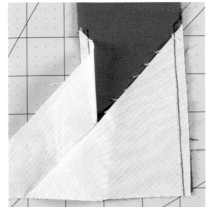

4 Sew a light fabric quarter-square triangle to each long side of a dark fabric rectangle to make a block side unit. Make (2) block side units. Align the quarter-square triangles with the bottom edge of the rectangle.
Note: There will be extra fabric at the top of the block side units.

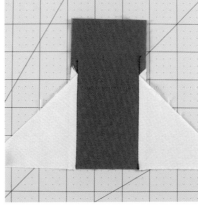

5 Press all seams toward the block side units.

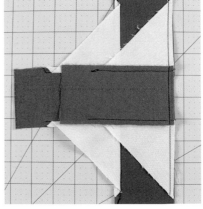

6 Pin the block side units to opposite sides of the block center strip, butting the seams as they cross the center square. Sew in place.

Method *continued*

 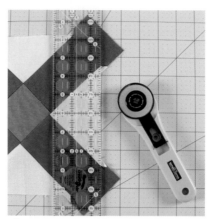 

7 Press the seams toward the block side units.

8 Trim the block to the desired size. Remember to include seam allowances when trimming. If you have a square ruler in the size needed for the finished block, lay it over the block with the center lines criss-crossing the seam intersections of the center square. Trim away the excess fabric to make an Album X block.

Sizing Charts

*wof indicates width of fabric

Album X Block

Finished size	Cut size	From 1 *wof strip you can get:
5" block	1-7/8" center squares	20
	1-7/8" x 3-1/2" rectangles	12
	4-1/4"squares for Quarter-square Triangles	9
6" block	2-1/4" center squares	16
	2-1/4" x 4-1/2" rectangles	9
	5" squares for Quarter-square Triangles	8
10" block	2-3/4" center squares	15
	2-3/4" x 5-1/1" rectangles	7
	6-1/4" squares for Quarter-square Triangles	6
12" block	3-3/8" center squares	10
	3-3/8" x 6-1/2" rectangles	6
	7 1/4" squares for Quarter-square Triangles	5

Album X Block

Finished size	Cut size	From 1 *wof strip you can get:
5" block	1-7/8" center squares	20
	1-7/8" x 3-1/2" rectangles	12
	4-1/4"squares for Quarter-square Triangles	9
6" block	2-1/4" center squares	16
	2-1/4" x 4-1/2" rectangles	9
	5" squares for Quarter-square Triangles	8
10" block	2-3/4" center squares	15
	2-3/4" x 5-1/1" rectangles	7
	6-1/4" squares for Quarter-square Triangles	6
12" block	3-3/8" center squares	10
	3-3/8" x 6-1/2" rectangles	6
	7-1/4" squarcs for Quarter-square Triangles	5

Setting Blocks on the Diagonal

Quilts with blocks set on the diagonal, such as those in the Diagonal Settings chapter beginning on page 74, need setting and corner triangles to complete the design. The triangles are cut from squares and the straight grain of the fabric should run up and down, as indicated by the arrows in the diagrams.

Setting Triangles

Setting triangles are placed on the outside edges of the quilt center to square it up. These triangles are sewn into rows with the blocks to create the quilt center.

To determine the size of the setting triangles, multiply the finished block size by 1.414 and add 1-1/4" for the seam allowances. Always round up to the nearest 1/8". Cut squares to the size determined and cut twice on the diagonal to make setting triangles.

Diagram 1 shows an example of the formula for making setting triangles.
A 9" finished block on the diagonal, or on point, measures 12-3/4" across the center. To determine the size of the setting triangles - 9" x 1.414 + 1-1/4" = 14" (rounded to the nearest 1/8")

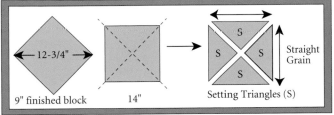

Diagram 1

Corner Triangles

Corner triangles are placed on the four outside corners of the quilt center to square it up after the blocks and setting triangles have been sewn together.

To determine the size of the corner triangles, divide the finished block size by 1.414 and add .875" (7/8") for the seam allowances. Always round up to the nearest 1/8". Cut squares to the size determined and cut once on the diagonal to make corner triangles.

Diagram 2 shows an example of the formula for making corner triangles.
A 9" finished block on the diagonal, or on point, measures 12-3/4" across the center. To determine the size of the corner triangles - 9" ÷ 1.414 + .875 = 7-1/4" (rounded to the nearest 1/8")

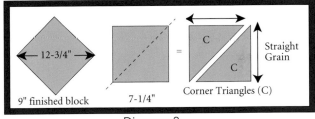

Diagram 2

For those of us who just want to know what size to cut our squares, the chart below gives the measurements to make setting and corner triangles for common block sizes.

Block Size	Diagonal Measurement	Square Size for Corner	Square Size for Setting
2"	2-7/8"	2-3/8"	4-1/8"
3"	4-1/4"	3"	5-1/2"
4"	5-5/8"	3-3/4"	6-7/8"
5"	7-1/8"	4-1/2"	8-3/8"
6"	8-1/2"	5-1/8"	9-3/4"
7"	9-7/8"	5-7/8"	11-1/8"
8"	11-3/8"	6-5/8"	12-5/8"
9"	12-3/4"	7-1/4"	14"
10"	14-1/8"	8"	15-3/8"
12"	17"	9-3/8"	18-1/4"
15"	21-1/4"	11-1/2"	22-1/2"
18"	25-1/2"	13-5/8"	26-3/4"

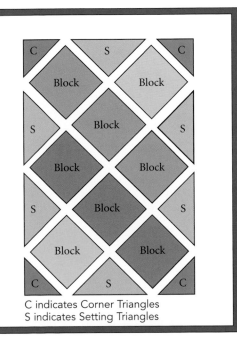

C indicates Corner Triangles
S indicates Setting Triangles

This Royal Stars quilt uses a popular star block with darker print fabrics in the corner triangles. A dark
color value was chosen to add the illusion of a Shoo Fly block around the sashing squares.
Further interest is incorporated into the design by the subtle use of a light background fabric in each
block, completing the transformation from a simple star quilt to an eye-catching overall design.

Basic Sashings

It is always best to start with the basics. Simple strip sashings made with the same fabric or contrasting sashing squares at the intersections of the quilt blocks is as basic as it gets. This type of setting is often chosen to sew a collection of quilt blocks together. However, a basic setting is just a starting point. Try manipulating colors and shapes within the blocks to create interesting quilt settings to make a quilt look fresh and original.

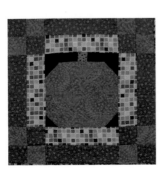

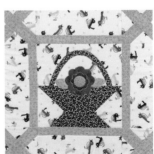

Royal Stars

Sashings can be used for more than just framing the blocks in a quilt. In the Royal Stars quilt the sashings are extended into the borders, taking the eye beyond the blocks and adding more interest to the overall quilt design.

Quilt designed by Jean Ann Wright; made by Cathy Francis.

Materials

Finished size approximately 26" x 26"

Royal Star blocks: 6" x 6"

wof indicates width of fabric

Note: Sew all blocks with a scant 1/4" seam and press all seams as you sew.

- Fabric A—1/2 yard black floral print (Royal Star blocks, sashings, border cornerstones)

- Fabric B—1/4 yard medium gold floral print (sashing squares, borders)

- Fabric C—1/4 yard moss green floral print (borders)

- Fabric D—1/4 yard pink leaf vine print (Royal Star blocks)

- Fabric E—1/4 yard rose red geometric print (Royal Star blocks)

- Fabric F—1/4 yard fern green geometric print (Royal Star blocks)

- Fabric G—1/8 yard light gold floral print (Royal Star blocks)

- Fabric H—1/8 yard light cream geometric print (Royal Star blocks)

- Fabric I—1/8 yard medium dark cream floral print (Royal Star blocks)

- Fabric J—1/2 yard red/black leaf print (Royal Star blocks, binding)

- Backing—1 yard

- Thread for machine quilting

- Crib or craft size batting

Note: Sulky® 40 wt Rayon #1829 Crème Brulée thread and Quilter's Dream® batting were used in this project.

Cutting Instructions

Fabric A, cut:
(3) 1-1/2" x wof strips, from these strips cut:
  (12) 1-1/2" x 6-1/2" sashing strips and
  (8) 1-1/2" x 3-1/2" sashing strips.

(1) 2-1/2" x wof strips, from this strip cut:
  (9) 2-1/2" squares.

(4) 1-1/2" x wof strips, from these strips cut:
  (72) 1-1/2" squares.

(1) 3-1/2" x wof strip, from this strip cut:
  (4) 3-1/2" border cornerstones.

Fabric B, cut:
(1) 3-1/2" x wof strip, from this strip cut:
  (4) 3-1/2" x 6-1/2" border rectangles.
From the remainder of the strip cut:
  (4) 1-1/2" sashing squares.

Fabric C, cut:
(2) 3-1/2" x wof strips, from these strips cut:
  (8) 3-1/2" x 6-1/2" border rectangles.

Fabric D, cut:
(4) 2-7/8" x wof strips, from these strips cut:
  (36) 2-7/8" squares.

Fabric E, cut:
(2) 2-7/8" x wof strips, from these strips cut:
  (18) 2-7/8" squares.

Fabric F, cut:
(2) 2-7/8" x wof strips, from these strips cut:
  (18) 2-7/8" squares.

Fabric G, cut:
(1) 2-1/2" x wof strip, from this strip cut:
  (12) 2-1/2" squares.

Fabric H, cut:
(1) 2-1/2" x wof strip, from this strip cut:
  (12) 2-1/2" squares.

Fabric I, cut:
(1) 2-1/2" x wof strip, from this strip cut:
  (12) 2-1/2" squares.

Fabric J, cut:
(2) 1-1/2" x wof strips, from these strips cut:
  (24) 1-1/2" squares.

(4) 2-1/4" x wof strips, sew together end-to-end for binding.

Block Assembly

Note: Refer to Half-square Triangles and Peaks directions on pages 9 and 16 to construct the blocks.

Royal Star blocks:

1. Lay a fabric J 1-1/2" square on one corner of a fabric I 2-1/2" square, right sides together, as shown. Sew a diagonal line across the 1-1/2" square and through the fabric layers.

2. Cut 1/4" away from the sewn line and press the seam allowance toward the triangle.

3. Lay a fabric J 1-1/2" square on the opposite side of the fabric I 2-1/2" square. Sew and press as before. Make (12) I Peaks units.

Make 12

4. Following steps 1 – 3 and using the fabric H 2-1/2" squares, the fabric G 2-1/2" squares and the fabric A 1-1/2" squares, make (12) H Peaks units and (12) G Peaks units.

Make 12   Make 12

5. To make the block corners draw a diagonal line from corner to corner on the wrong side of the fabric D 2-7/8" squares.

6. Lay half of the marked squares on the (18) fabric E 2-7/8" squares, right sides together. Stitch 1/4" on each side of the drawn line. Cut apart on the drawn line. Press the seam allowance toward the darker fabric. Make (18) D/E half-square triangles.

Make 18

7. Repeat step 6 using the remaining marked fabric D squares and the fabric F 2-7/8" squares. Make (18) D/F half-square triangles.

Make 18

8. Join matching Peaks units to opposite sides of the (9) 2-1/2" fabric A squares as shown. Take care to match the Peak units with the same background color. Make (3) units in each color scheme for a total of (9) units.

Make 3   Make 3   Make 3

9. Referring to the diagram below for placement, join the half-square triangle units to opposite sides of the remaining Peaks units. Make (6) units in each colorway for a total of (18) units.

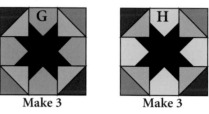

Make 6   Make 6   Make 6

10. Sew the units made in step 8 to opposite sides of the units made in step 9, matching the background fabrics in each block. Make (3) blocks in matching background fabrics for a total of (9) Royal Star blocks.

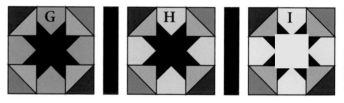

Make 3   Make 3   Make 3

Block Row Assembly

Lay out (3) Royal Star blocks and (2) fabric A 1-1/2" x 6-1/2" sashing strips as shown. Sew together to make a block row. Make (3) block rows. Refer to the Quilt Assembly Diagram to position the blocks with different background fabrics in each row.

Sashing Rows

Lay out (3) fabric A 1-1/2" x 6-1/2" sashing strips and (2) fabric B 1-1/2" squares as shown. Sew together to make a sashing row. Make (2) sashing rows.

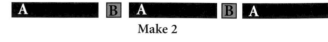

Make 2

Quilt Center Assembly

Referring to the Quilt Assembly Diagram, lay out the (3) block rows and the (2) sashing rows. Sew together to complete the quilt center.

Borders

1. Sew a fabric A 1-1/2" x 3-1/2" sashing strip to each end of a fabric B 3-1/2" x 6-1/2" border rectangle. Sew a fabric C 3-1/2" x 6-1/2" border rectangle to the end of the fabric A sashing strips to make a pieced border. Make (4) pieced borders.

2. Sew a pieced border to opposite sides of the quilt center.

3. Referring to the Quilt Assembly Diagram, sew a fabric A 3-1/2" cornerstone square to each end of the two remaining pieced borders. Sew these borders to the top and bottom of the quilt center.

Finishing the Quilt

Layer the quilt backing fabric, batting and quilt top. Baste the layers together. Hand or machine quilt as desired. Bind to finish the quilt.

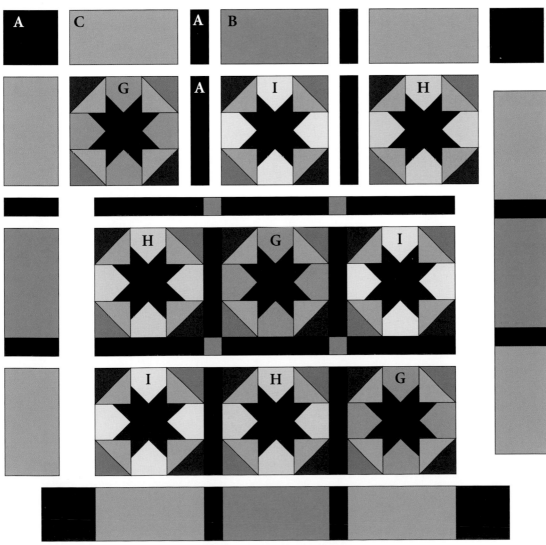

Quilt Assembly Diagram

Double Nine Patch

A Nine Patch block is simple and basic, but there are dozens of designs that can be created when you play with it. The Double Nine Patch blocks in this quilt are made from small Nine Patches sewn into a larger Nine Patch. Additional small Nine Patches are used as setting squares in the pieced sashing rows to create an allover mosaic pattern that resembles an Irish chain design. Try substituting another block in place of the Nine Patch for a completely different look.

Quilt designed and made by Jean Ann Wright.

30

Materials

Finished size approximately 35" x 47"

Double Nine Patch blocks: 9" x 9"

wof indicates width of fabric

Note: Sew all blocks with a scant 1/4" seam and press all seams as you sew.

- Fabric A—2/3 yard brown print (borders)

- Fabric B—1/4 yard blue print (Double Nine Patch blocks)

- Fabric C—1/3 yard muslin small print (Nine Patch blocks)

- Fabric D—3/4 yard dark brown small print (Nine Patch blocks, binding)

- Fabric E—2/3 yard light beige print (sashings)

- Fabric F—1/3 yard brick red print (sashings)

- Backing—1-1/4 yards

- Thread for machine quilting

- Crib or craft size batting

Note: Sulky® 30 wt Blendables® #4010 Caramel Apple thread and Quilter's Dream® Green batting were used in this project.

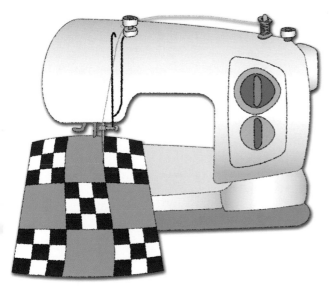

Cutting Instructions

Fabric A, cut:
(4) 4-1/2" x wof strips, from these strips cut:
　(2) 4-1/2" x 39-1/2" side border strips and
　(2) 4-1/2" x 35-1/2" top/bottom border strips.

Fabric B, cut:
(2) 3-1/2" x wof strips, from these strips cut:
　(24) 3-1/2" squares.

Fabric C, cut:
(7) 1-1/2" x wof strips.

Fabric D, cut:
(8) 1-1/2" x wof strips.

(4) 2-1/4" x wof strips, sew together end-to-end for binding.

Fabric E, cut:
(12) 1-1/2" x wof strips.

Fabric F, cut:
(6) 1-1/2" x wof strips.

Block Assembly

Note: Refer to Nine Patch block directions on page 19 to construct the block.

Nine Patch blocks:

1. Sew together (2) fabric D 1-1/2" x wof strips and (1) fabric C 1-1/2" x wof strip, as shown, to make strip set A. Press seams toward fabric D. Repeat to make a total of (3) strip set A.

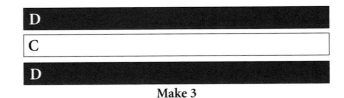

Make 3

2. Crosscut each strip set A into 1-1/2"-wide segments. Make (84) D-C-D units.

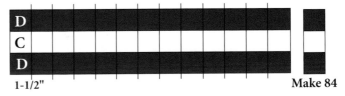

1-1/2"　　　　　　　　　　　　　Make 84

3. Sew together (2) fabric C 1-1/2" x wof strips and (1) fabric D 1-1/2" x wof strip, as shown, to make strip set B. Press seams toward fabric D. Repeat to make a total of (2) strip set B. Crosscut each strip set B into 1-1/2"-wide segments. Make (42) C-D-C units.

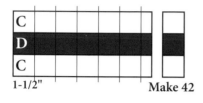

Make 42

4. Sew (2) D-C-D units and (1) C-D-C unit together to make a Nine Patch block. Make (42) Nine Patch blocks.

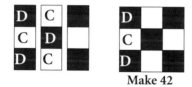

Make 42

Double Nine Patch blocks:

Lay out (5) Nine Patch blocks and (4) fabric B 3-1/2" squares, as shown, and sew together to make a Double Nine Patch block. Make (6) Double Nine Patch blocks. You will have (12) Nine Patch blocks left over. Set these aside for the sashing rows.

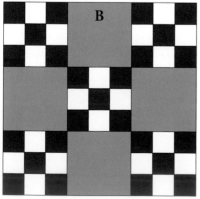

Make 6

Sashings

Sew a fabric E 1-1/2" x wof strip to each side of a fabric F 1-1/2" x wof strip. Press seams toward fabric F. Make (6) strip sets. Crosscut the E-F-E strip sets at 10-1/4" intervals to make (17) pieced sashing units.

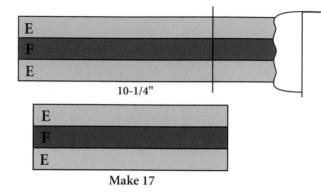

10-1/4"

Make 17

Sashing Row Assembly

Alternate (3) Nine Patch blocks with (2) pieced sashing units to make a sashing row. Make (4) sashing rows.

Make 4

Block Row Assembly

Alternate (3) pieced sashing units with (2) Double Nine Patch blocks to make a block row. Make (3) block rows.

Make 3

Quilt Center Assembly

Referring to the Quilt Assembly Diagram, lay out the (4) sashing rows and the (3) block rows as shown. Join the rows together to complete the quilt center. Press seams toward the sashing rows.

Borders

Join the fabric A 4-1/2" x 39-1/2" side border strips to opposite sides of the quilt center. Press seams toward the borders. Join the fabric A 4-1/2" x 35-1/2" top/bottom border strips to the top/bottom of the quilt center. Press seams toward the borders.

Finishing the Quilt

Layer the quilt backing fabric, batting and quilt top. Baste the layers together. Hand or machine quilt as desired. Bind to finish the quilt.

A

Quilt Assembly Diagram

Birdsong

Quilts with especially interesting blocks call for simplicity in the sashings. In the Birdsong quilt, the Thrift blocks are fussy cut and the largest triangles in the block are placed to give the illusion of a strong vertical stripe. A very basic setting of simple sashings and cornerstones lets the blocks sing.

Quilt designed and made by Jean Ann Wright.

34

Materials

Finished size approximately 74" x 88"

Thrift blocks: 12" x 12"

wof indicates width of fabric

Note: Sew all blocks with a scant 1/4" seam and press all seams as you sew.

- Fabric A—2-5/8 yards blue/brown rose bouquet print (outer borders, cornerstone blocks, binding)

- Fabric B—2 yards brown/white bird print (Thrift blocks)

- Fabric C—1 yard brown/white floral print (Thrift blocks)

- Fabric D—1 yard white/pink twisted ribbons print (Thrift blocks)

- Fabric E—1 yard blue/brown twisted ribbons print (Thrift blocks)

- Fabric F—1-1/2 yards pink geometric print (sashing, inner borders, cornerstone blocks)

- Fabric G—1/3 yard blue small flower print (sashing squares, cornerstone blocks)

- Backing—5 yards

- Thread for machine quilting

- Queen size batting

Note: Sulky® 30 wt Blendables® #4036 Earth Taupes thread and Quilter's Dream Orient® batting were used in this project.

Cutting Instructions

Fabric A, cut:
(7) 8-1/2" x wof strips, sew together end-to-end and cut:
    (2) 8-1/2" x 72-1/2" side outer border strips and
    (2) 8-1/2" x 58-1/2" top/bottom outer border strips.

From leftover fabric, fussy cut: (4) 4-1/2" squares.

Cut (9) 2-1/4" x wof strips,
    sew together end-to-end for binding.

Fabric B, fussy cut:
(20) 6-1/2" squares centering a bird motif in each square. (yardage may need to be increased depending on number of motifs that can be cut from a yard of fabric)

Fabric C, cut:
(4) 7-1/4" x wof strips, from these strips cut:
    (20) 7-1/4" squares; cut each square in half on the diagonal twice to make (80) quarter-square triangles.

Fabric D, cut:
(4) 6-7/8" x wof strips, from these strips cut:
    (20) 6-7/8" squares; cut each square in half on the diagonal once to make (40) half-square triangles.

Fabric E, cut:
(4) 6-7/8" x wof strips, from these strips cut:
    (20) 6-7/8" squares; cut each square in half on the diagonal once to make (40) half-square triangles.

Fabric F, cut:
(2) 12-1/2" x wof strips, from these strips cut:
    (31) 12-1/2" x 2-1/2" sashing strips.

(7) 2-1/2" x wof strips,
    sew together end-to-end and cut:
    (2) 2-1/2" x 68-1/2" side inner border strips and
    (2) 2-1/2" x 58-1/2" top/bottom inner border strips.

(1) 4-7/8" x wof strip, from this strip cut:
    (8) 4-7/8" squares; cut each square in half on the diagonal once to make (16) half-square triangles.

Fabric G, cut:
(1) 2-1/2" x wof strip, from this strip cut:
    (12) 2-1/2" x 2-1/2" sashing squares.

(1) 5-1/4" x wof strip, from this strip cut:
    (4) 5-1/4" squares; cut each square in half on the diagonal twice to make (16) quarter-square triangles.

Block Assembly

Note: Refer to Thrift block directions on page 20 to construct the blocks.

Block A:

Lay a fabric C 7-1/4" quarter-square triangle on each side of a fabric B 6-1/2" square, right sides together, and sew in place. Position (2) fabric D 6-7/8" half-square triangles on the left side of the block and (2) fabric E 6-7/8" half-square triangles on the right side of the block. Sew in place to complete Block A. Make (10) Block A.

Make 10

Block B:

Lay a fabric C 7-1/4" quarter-square triangle on each side of a fabric B 6-1/2" square, right sides together, and sew in place. Position (2) fabric E 6-7/8" half-square triangles on the left side of the block and (2) fabric D 6-7/8" half-square triangles on the right side of the block. Sew in place to complete Block B. Make (10) Block B.

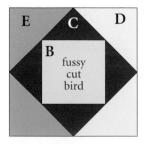

Make 10

Cornerstone blocks:

Sew a fabric G 5-1/4" quarter-square triangle to each side of a fabric A fussy cut 4-1/2" square. Sew a fabric F 4-7/8" half-square triangle to each side of the fabric G triangles to complete the Cornerstone block. Make (4) Cornerstone blocks.

Make 4

Block Row Assembly

Lay out (2) Block A, (2) Block B and (3) fabric F 2-1/2" x 12-1/2" sashing strips as shown. Sew the pieces together in this order: Block A, sashing strip, Block B, sashing strip, Block A, sashing strip and Block B to make a block row. Make (5) block rows.

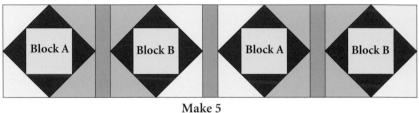

Make 5

Sashing Row Assembly

Lay out (4) 2-1/2" x 12-1/2" fabric F sashing strips and (3) 2-1/2" fabric G sashing squares in a row. Sew the pieces together to form a sashing row. Make (4) sashing rows.

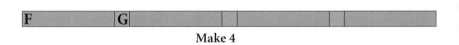

Make 4

Quilt Center Assembly

Following the Quilt Assembly Diagram, lay out the (5) block rows and the (4) sashing rows. Sew the rows together to complete the quilt center.

Inner Border

Sew the fabric F 2-1/2" x 68-1/2" side inner border strips to opposite sides of the quilt center. Press seams toward the borders. Sew the fabric F 2-1/2" x 58-1/2" top/bottom inner border strips to the top/bottom of the quilt center. Press seams toward the borders.

Outer Border

Sew the fabric A 8-1/2" x 72-1/2" side outer border strips to opposite sides of the quilt center. Press seams toward the borders. Sew a Cornerstone block to each side of the fabric A 8-1/2" x 58-1/2" top/bottom outer border strips. Sew these borders to the top/bottom of the quilt center to complete the quilt. Press seams toward the borders.

Finishing the Quilt

Layer the backing fabric, batting and quilt top. Baste the layers together. Hand or machine quilt as desired. Bind to finish the quilt.

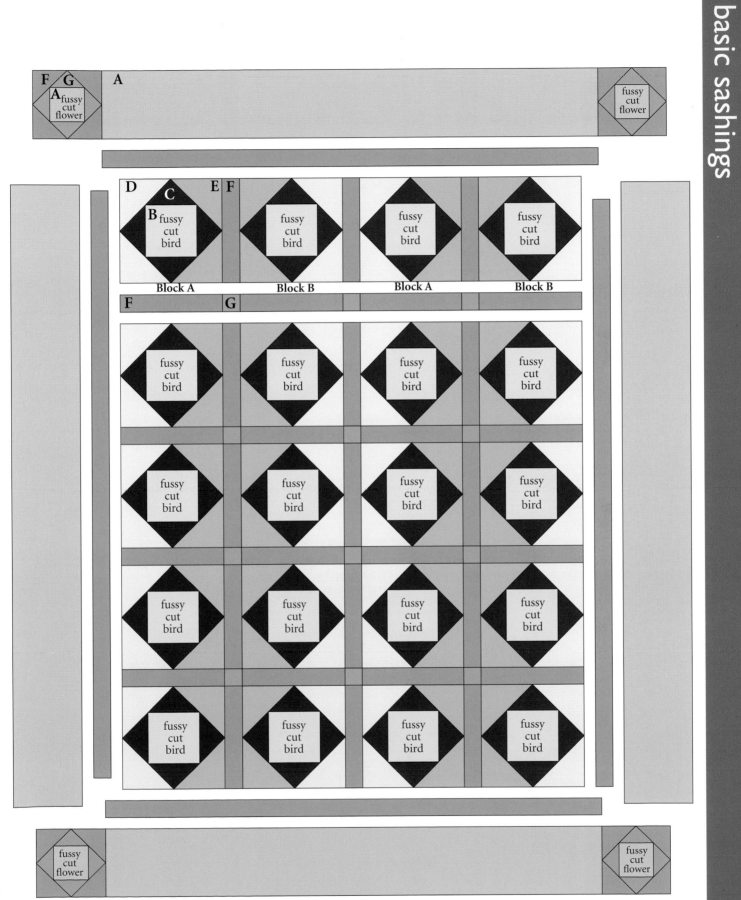

Quilt Assembly Diagram

Playful Pinwheels

Don't be afraid to use traditional blocks as part of your quilt's sashing. Pinwheel block setting squares are sewn to rectanglar sashing strips. They combine with the Crossroads to Jericho block rows to create an interesting and imaginative quilt setting.

Quilt designed and made by Jean Ann Wright.

Materials

Finished size approximately 49-1/2" x 65-1/4"

Crossroads to Jericho blocks: 9-3/4" x 9-3/4"

Pinwheel blocks: 6" x 6"

wof indicates width of fabric

Note: Sew all blocks with a scant 1/4" seam and press all seams as you sew.

- Fabric A—1-1/4 yards multi-color stripe print (borders)
- Fabric B—1-1/2 yards cream texture print fabric (sashings, binding)
- Fabric C—1/2 yard blue texture print (Pinwheel blocks)
- Fabric D—3/4 yard yellow texture print (Pinwheel and Nine Patch blocks)
- Fabric E—1/4 yard red texture print (Nine Patch blocks)
- Fabric F—1/3 yard light green texture print (Crossroads to Jericho blocks)
- Backing—3-1/4 yards
- Thread for machine quilting
- Crib or craft size batting

Note: Sulky® 30 wt Blendables® #4124 Summertime thread and Quilter's Dream® batting were used in this project.

Cutting Instructions

Fabric A, cut:
(6) 6-1/2" x wof strips, sew together end-to-end and cut:
(2) 6-1/2" x 57-3/4" side border strips and (2) 6-1/2" x 50" top/bottom border strips.

Fabric B, cut:
(5) 6-1/2" x wof strips, from these strips cut:
(17) 6-1/2" x 10-1/4" sashing strips.

(6) 2-1/4" x wof strips, sew together end-to-end for binding.

Fabric C, cut:
(3) 3-7/8" x wof strips, from these strips cut:
(24) 3-7/8" squares.

Fabric D, cut:
(3) 3-7/8" x wof strips, from these strips cut:
(24) 3-7/8" squares.

(3) 2-1/2" x wof strips.

Fabric E, cut:
(3) 2-1/2" x wof strips.

Fabric F, cut:
(2) 5-1/8" x wof strips, from these strips cut:
(12) 5-1/8" squares; cut each square in half once on the diagonal to make (24) half-square triangles.

Block Assembly

Note: Refer to the Half-square Triangles and Nine Patch block directions on pages 9 and 19 to construct the blocks.

Pinwheel blocks:

1. Draw a diagonal line from corner to corner on the wrong side of the (24) fabric D 3-7/8" squares. Layer a fabric D 3-7/8" square and a fabric C 3-7/8" square, right sides together. Stitch 1/4" on each side of the drawn line. Cut apart on the drawn line. Press both seams toward fabric C to complete the half-square triangle. Make (48) half-square triangles.

Make 48

2. Sew together (4) half-square triangles, as shown, to make a Pinwheel block. Make (12) Pinwheel blocks.

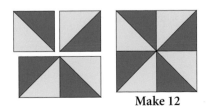

Make 12

39

Nine Patch blocks:

1. Sew (2) fabric E 2-1/2" x wof strips and (1) fabric D 2-1/2" x wof strip together as shown. Press seams toward fabric E to make (1) strip set A.

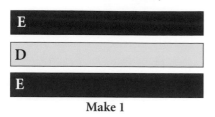

Make 1

2. Crosscut strip set A into 2-1/2" segments. Make (12) E-D-E units.

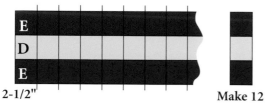

2-1/2"   **Make 12**

3. Sew together (2) fabric D 2-1/2" x wof strips and (1) fabric E 2-1/2" x wof strip as shown. Press seams toward fabric E to make (1) strip set B.

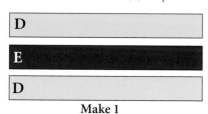

Make 1

4. Crosscut strip set B into 2-1/2" segments to make (6) D-E-D units.

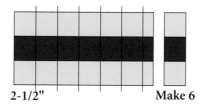

2-1/2"   **Make 6**

5. Sew (2) E-D-E units and (1) D-E-D unit together as shown to make a Nine Patch block. Make (6) Nine Patch blocks.

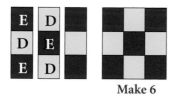

Make 6

Crossroads to Jericho blocks

Sew a fabric F 5-1/8" half-square triangle to each side of a Nine Patch block to make a Crossroads to Jericho block. Press seams toward the half-square triangles. Make (6) Crossroads to Jericho blocks.

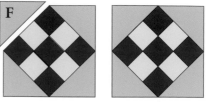

Make 6

Pinwheel Block Row Assembly

Following the Quilt Assembly Diagram, lay out (3) Pinwheel blocks and (2) fabric B 6-1/2" x 10-1/4" sashing strips in a row. Sew the pieces together to make a Pinwheel block row. Make (4) Pinwheel block rows.

Crossroads to Jericho Block Row Assembly

Following the Quilt Assembly Diagram, lay out (3) fabric B 6-1/2" x 10-1/4" sashing strips and (2) Crossroads to Jericho blocks in a row. Sew the pieces together to make a Crossroads to Jericho block row. Make (3) Crossroads to Jericho block rows.

Quilt Center Assembly

Following the Quilt Assembly Diagram, lay out the (4) Pinwheel block rows and the (3) Crossroads to Jericho block rows, as shown, to complete the quilt center. Press seams in one direction.

Border

Sew the fabric A 6-1/2" x 57-3/4" side border strips to opposite sides of the quilt center. Press seams toward the borders. Join the fabric A 6-1/2" x 50" top/bottom border strips to the top/bottom of the quilt center. Press seams toward the borders.

Finishing the Quilt

Layer the backing fabric, batting and quilt top. Baste the layers together. Hand or machine quilt as desired. Bind to finish the quilt.

A

B

B

Quilt Assembly Diagram

Spring Table Runner

Rail Fence sashings and Album X sashing squares frame the appliqué blocks in this seasonal table runner. Substitute snowmen or fall leaves in another colorway for the flowers and baskets to create an autumn or winter look for your table.

Materials

Finished size approximately 20" x 50"

Basket blocks: 10" x 10"

wof indicates width of fabric.

Note: Sew all blocks with a scant 1/4" seam and press all seams as you sew.

- Fabric A—1 yard white whimsical print (Basket and Album X blocks, sashings)

- Fabric B—1 yard green print (Album X blocks, flower appliqués, sashings, binding)

- Fabric C—1/3 yard geometric print (Basket blocks)

- Fabric D—1/8 yard orange (flower appliqués)

- Fabric E—1/8 yard purple (flower appliqués)

- Fabric F—1/8 yard gold (flower appliqués)

- Backing—1-1/2 yards

- Thread for machine quilting

- Invisible thread for appliqué

- Craft size batting

- Temporary spray adhesive or fusible web for appliqué

Note: Sulky® 40 wt rayon thread #1002 soft white thread, Sulky® invisible thread, Sulky® KK2000 Temporary Spray Adhesive and Quilter's Dream® Green batting were used in this project.

Table Runner designed and made by Jean Ann Wright.

Cutting Instructions

Fabric A, cut:

(3) 3-1/2" x wof strips, from these strips cut:
   (10) 3-1/2" x 10-1/2" sashing strips.

(1) 10-1/2" x wof strip, from this strip cut:
   (1) 10-1/2" square.
   Trim the remainder of the strip to 5-1/2" and cut:
   (2) 5-1/2" x 10-1/2" rectangles.

(1) 4-1/4" x wof strip, from this strip cut:
   (8) 4-1/4" squares; cut each square in half on the diagonal twice to make
   (32) quarter-square triangles.

(1) 5-7/8" x wof strip, from this strip cut:
   (2) 5-7/8" squares; cut each square in half on the diagonal once to make (4) half-square triangles.

Fabric B, cut:

(5) 1-1/2" x wof strips, from these strips cut:
   (20) 1-1/2" x 10-1/2" sashing strips.

(4) 1-7/8" x wof strips, from these strips cut:
   (32) 1-7/8" x 3-3/4" rectangles and
   (8) 1-7/8" squares

(4) 2-1/4" x wof strips, sew together end-to-end for binding.

From the remaining green print, cut (6) large leaves,
   (6) small leaves,
   (2) large stems and (2) small stems using the templates on page 47.

Fabric C, cut:

(1) 11-1/4" square; cut the square in half on the diagonal once to make (2) basket base pieces.

(2) 3-7/8" squares; cut the squares in half on the diagonal to make (4) basket base pieces.

(2) basket handles using the template on page 46.

Fabric D, cut:

(4) large flowers using the template on page 47.

Fabric E, cut:

(4) small flowers using the template on page 47.

(2) flower buds using the template on page 47.

Fabric F, cut:

(4) flower centers using the template on page 47.

Block Assembly

Note: Refer to Album X block directions on page 21 to construct the sashing squares.

Basket blocks:

1. Center a basket handle on a fabric A 5-1/2" x 10-1/2" rectangle. Adhere the handle to the rectangle using spray adhesive or fusible web. Sew the handle in place with a narrow zigzag stitch and invisible thread. Make (2) basket handle blocks and set aside.

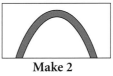

Make 2

2. Pin a fabric C 3-7/8" quarter-square triangle to a fabric C 11-1/4" half-square triangle, right sides together, as shown. Lay a fabric A 5-7/8" half-square triangle on top of the fabric C triangle, right sides together. Sew along the edge. Press the seams away from the 11-1/4" half-square triangle. Appliqué the fabric C quarter-square triangle to the fabric A half-square triangle.

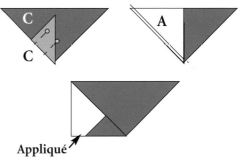

Appliqué

3. Repeat on the remaining side to finish the basket base. Make (2) basket base blocks.

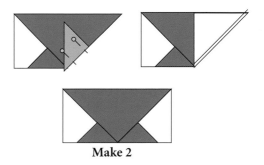

Make 2

43

4. Sew a basket handle and a basket base block together as shown to make a Basket block. Make (2) Basket blocks.

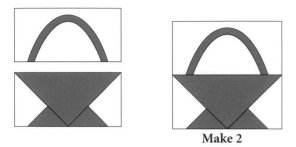

Make 2

5. Referring to the diagram, appliqué the flower and leaves in place on the Basket blocks.

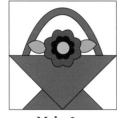

Make 2

Center block:

Referring to the diagram, position the remaining appliqué pieces on the fabric A 10-1/2" square. Appliqué the pieces in place to complete the Center block.

Album X sashing squares:

1. Sew a fabric B 1-7/8" x 3-3/4" rectangle to opposite sides of a fabric B 1-7/8" square. Press seams toward the square. Make (8) B strips.

Make 8

2. Sew a fabric A 4-1/4" quarter-square triangle to opposite sides of a fabric B 1-7/8" x 3-3/4" rectangle. Keep the base of the quarter-square triangles aligned with one end of the fabric B rectangle, as shown. Press seams toward the rectangle. Make (16) A/B triangle units.

Make 16

3. Pin an A/B triangle unit and a B strip together, matching the center seams. Sew the two pieces together. Press seams toward the A/B triangle unit. Sew an A/B triangle unit to the opposite side of the B strip to complete the Album X sashing square. Make (8) Album X sashing squares.

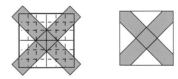

Make 8

4. Trim the sashing squares to 5-1/2" x 5-1/2" using a square ruler and aligning the center marks on the ruler with the center of the block.

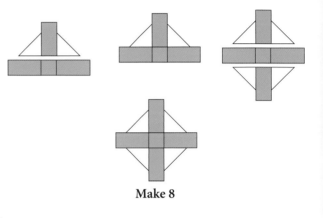

Sashing Assembly

Sew a fabric B 1-1/2" x 10-1/2" sashing strip to opposite sides of a fabric A 3-1/2" x 10-1/2" sashing strip to make a pieced sashing strip. Make (10) pieced sashing strips.

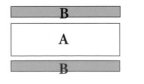

Make 10

Table Runner Assembly

Referring to the Table Runner Assembly Diagram, sew a pieced sashing strip to opposite sides of the (2) Basket blocks and the Center block. Sew an Album X sashing square to each side of the remaining (4) pieced sashing strips. Alternate the sashing rows and the block rows to complete the table runner.

Finishing the Table Runner

Layer the backing fabric, batting and table runner top. Baste the layers together. Hand or machine quilt as desired. Bind to finish the table runner.

Table Runner Assembly Diagram

45

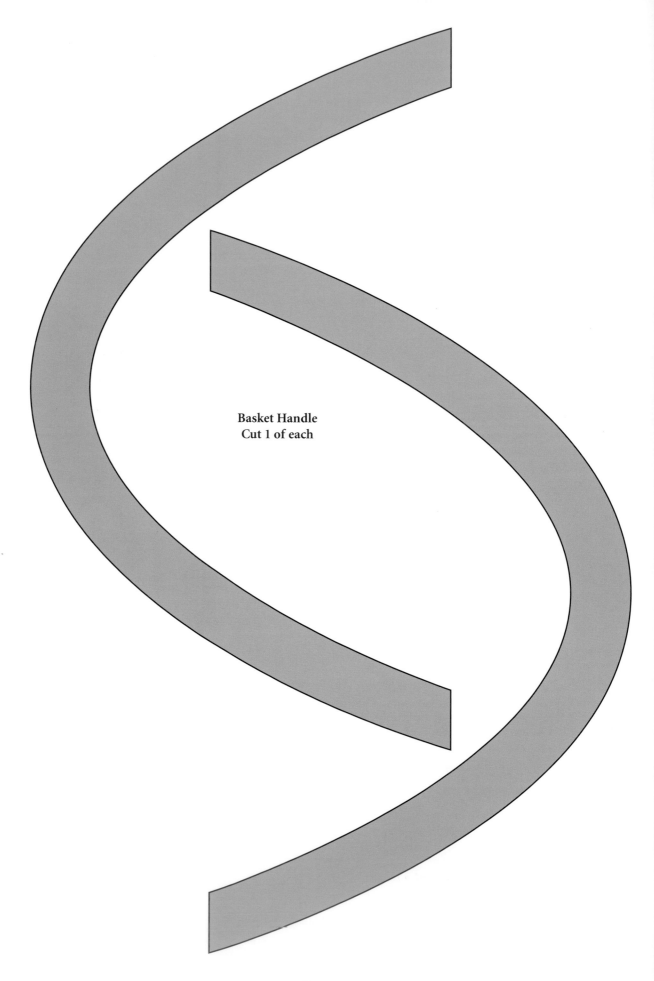

Basket Handle
Cut 1 of each

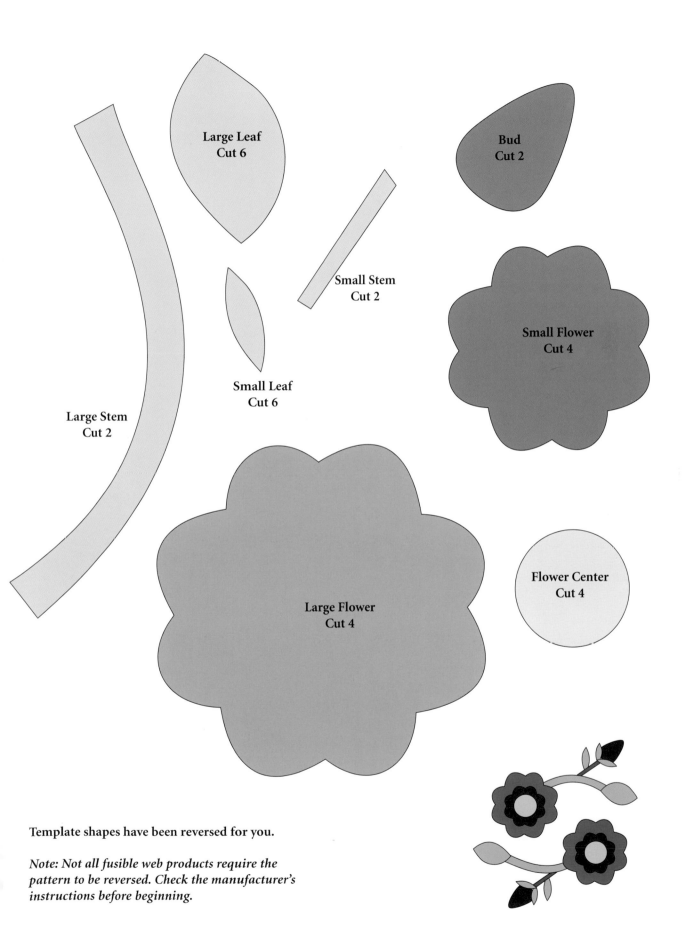

Large Leaf
Cut 6

Bud
Cut 2

Small Stem
Cut 2

Small Flower
Cut 4

Small Leaf
Cut 6

Large Stem
Cut 2

Flower Center
Cut 4

Large Flower
Cut 4

Template shapes have been reversed for you.

Note: Not all fusible web products require the pattern to be reversed. Check the manufacturer's instructions before beginning.

Summer Table Runner

The pieced sashings in this table runner are created using small squares in an alternating checkerboard design. The look enhances the idea of a summer picnic. Sashings that build on the design theme of the blocks are always successful.

Table Runner designed and made by Jean Ann Wright.

Materials

Finished size approximately 22" x 46"

Cross Patch blocks: 10" x 10"

wof indicates width of fabric

Note: Sew all blocks with a scant 1/4" seam and press all seams as you sew.

- Fabric A—1 yard watermelon print (Cross Patch blocks, borders)

- Fabric B—1/2 yard red/white check with ants (sashings, binding)

- Fabric C—1/4 yard lime green mini-print (Cross Patch blocks)

- Fabric D—1/4 yard white print (sashings)

- Fabric E—1/4 yard black print (sashings)

- Backing—1-1/2 yards

- Thread for machine quilting

- Craft size batting

Note: Sulky® 40 wt Rayon #1039 true red thread and Quilter's Dream® Green batting were used in this project.

Cutting Instructions

Fabric A, cut:
(5) 4-1/2" x wof strips, from these strips cut:
    (2) 4-1/2" x 38-1/2" side border strips and
    (2) 4-1/2" x 22-1/2" top/bottom border strips.
    From the remaining strip and the remainder of
    the top/bottom border strips cut:
    (12) 4-1/2" squares.

Fabric B, cut:
(1) 2-1/2" x wof strip, from this strip cut:
    (11) 2-1/2" squares.

(4) 2-1/4" x wof strips, sew together end-to-end
    for binding.

Fabric C, cut:
(2) 2-1/2" x wof strips, from these strips cut:
    (12) 2-1/2" x 4-1/2" rectangles.

Fabric D, cut:
(2) 2-1/2" x wof strips, from these strips cut:
    (30) 2-1/2" squares.

Fabric E, cut:
(2) 2-1/2" x wof strips, from this strip cut:
    (20) 2-1/2" squares.

Cross Patch Block Assembly

1. Sew a fabric A 4-1/2" square to opposite sides of a fabric C 2-1/2" x 4-1/2" rectangle to make an A/C unit. Make (6) A/C units.

Make 6

2. Sew a fabric C 2-1/2" x 4-1/2" rectangle to opposite sides of a fabric B 2-1/2" square to make a B/C unit. Make (3) B/C units.

Make 3

3. Sew an A/C unit to each side of a B/C unit to make a Cross Patch block. Make (3) Cross Patch blocks.

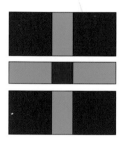 

Make 3

Sashing Assembly

Lay out (3) fabric D 2-1/2" squares and (2) fabric E 2-1/2" squares. Sew the square together to make a pieced sashing strip. Make (10) pieced sashing strips.

Make 10

Table Runner Assembly

1. Sew a pieced sashing strip to each side of the (3) Cross Patch blocks.

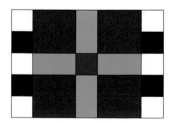

2. Sew a fabric B 2-1/2" square to each end of the remaining (4) sashing strips.

Make 4

3. Referring to the Table Runner Assembly Diagram, lay out the (4) sashing strips and the (3) Cross Patch blocks. Sew together to make the table runner center.

Borders

1. Referring to the Table Runner Assembly Diagram, sew the fabric A 4-1/2" x 38-1/2" side border strips to opposite sides of the table runner center.

2. Sew the fabric A 4-1/2" x 22-1/2" top/bottom border strips to the top/bottom of the table runner center.

Finishing the Table Runner

Layer the backing fabric, batting and table runner top. Baste the layers together. Hand or machine quilt as desired. Bind to finish the table runner.

Table Runner Assembly Diagram

Autumn Table Runner

Sashing strip sets and four patch blocks highlight the blocks in this design and give the eye a resting place.

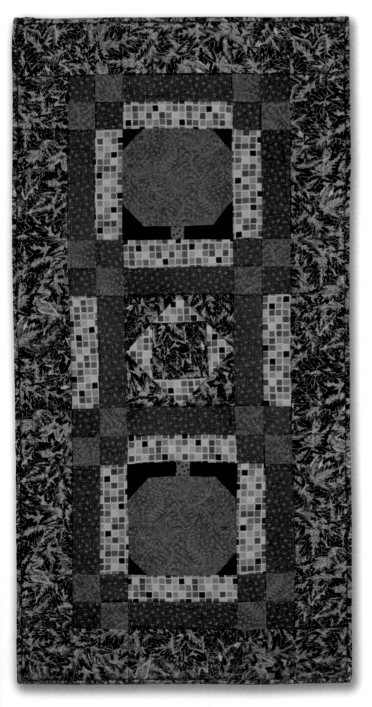

Table Runner designed and made by Jean Ann Wright.

Materials

Finished size approximately 24" x 48"

Thrift block: 8" x 8"

Pumpkin blocks: 8" x 8"

wof indicates width of fabric

Note: Sew all blocks with a scant 1/4" seam and press all seams as you sew.

- Fabric A—1 yard autumn leaf print (Thrift block, borders, binding)

- Fabric B—1/2 yard multi-check print (Thrift block, sashings)

- Fabric C—1/4 yard olive green mini-print (sashings, Four Patch setting squares)

- Fabric D—1/3 yard orange print (Pumpkin blocks, Four Patch setting squares)

- Fabric E—1/8 yard dark brown (Pumpkin blocks)

- Fabric F—scrap light print (Pumpkin blocks)

- Backing—1-1/2 yards

- Thread for machine quilting

- Craft size batting

Note: Sulky® 40 wt Rayon #1174 dark pine green thread and Quilter's Dream® Green batting were used in this project.

Cutting Instructions

Fabric A, cut:

(4) 4-1/2" x wof strips, sew together end-to-end then cut:
  (2) 4-1/2" x 40-1/2" side border strips and
  (2) 4-1/2" x 24-1/2" top/bottom border strips.

(1) 4-7/8" x wof strip, from this strip cut:
  (2) 4-7/8" squares; cut each square in half on the diagonal once to make
  (4) half-square triangles.
  From the remainder of the 4-7/8" strip, cut
  (1) 4-1/2" square.

(4) 2-1/4" x wof strips, sew together end-to-end for binding.

Fabric B, cut:

(2) 2-1/2" x wof strips, from these strips cut:
  (10) 2-1/2" x 8-1/2" sashing strips.

(1) 5-1/4" square; cut the square in
  half on the diagonal twice to make
  (4) quarter-square triangles.

Fabric C, cut:

(3) 2-1/2" x wof strips, from these strips cut:
  (10) 2-1/2" x 8-1/2" sashing strips and
  (16) 2-1/2" squares.

Fabric D, cut:

(1) 7-1/2" x wof strip, from this strip cut:
  (2) 7-1/2" x 8-1/2" rectangles.
  Cut the remainder of the 7-1/2" strip into
  (3) 2-1/2" strips, from these strips cut:
  (16) 2-1/2" squares.

Fabric E, cut:

(1) 1-1/2" x wof strip, from this strip cut:
  (4) 1-1/2" x 4" strips.

(1) 2" x wof strip, from this strip cut:
  (8) 2" squares.

Fabric F, cut:

(2) 1-1/2" squares for pumpkin stems.

Block Assembly

Note: Refer to Thrift block directions on page 20 to construct the block.

Thrift block:

1. Lay a fabric B 5-1/4" quarter-square triangle on opposite sides of the fabric A 4-1/2" square, right sides together, and sew in place. Press seams toward the triangles. Lay a fabric B 5-1/4" quarter-square triangle on the remaining sides of the fabric A 4-1/2" square. Sew in place. Press the seams toward the triangles to make a center unit.

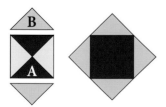

2. Lay a fabric A 4-7/8" half-square triangle on opposite sides of the center unit, right sides together, and sew in place. Press seams toward the triangles. Lay a fabric A 4-7/8" half-square triangle on the remaining sides of the center unit and sew in place. Press the seams toward the triangles to make a Thrift block.

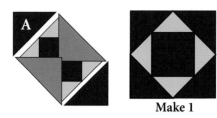

Make 1

Pumpkin blocks:

1. Lay a fabric E 2" square in each corner of a fabric D 7-1/2" x 8-1/2" rectangle, right sides together. Stitch in a diagonal line across the 2" fabric square through the fabric layers. Trim 1/4" away from the sewn line and press the triangles open to make the pumpkin. Make (2) pumpkins.

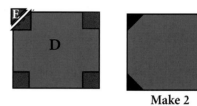

Make 2

2. Sew a fabric E 1-1/2" x 4" strip to each side of a fabric F 1-1/2" square to make a narrow strip. Make (2) narrow strips.

Make 2

3. Sew a narrow strip to each pumpkin to complete the block. Make (2) Pumpkin blocks.

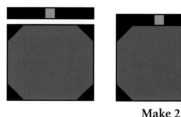

Make 2

Sashing Assembly

1. Sew a fabric B 2-1/2" x 8-1/2" sashing strip to a fabric C 2-1/2" x 8-1/2" sashing strip to make a B/C sashing unit. Make (10) B/C sashing units.

Make 10

2. Layer a fabric C 2-1/2" square and a fabric D 2-1/2" square, right sides together. Sew the squares together along one side. Press squares open. Continue until all the squares have been sewn together in pairs. Make (16) pairs.

Make 16

3. Layer the pairs, right sides together, with the fabric D squares on the fabric C squares. Sew the pairs together and press open to make a Four Patch block. Make (8) Four Patch blocks.

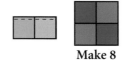

Make 8

4. Sew a Four Patch block to each end of (4) B/C sashing units, positioning the orange against the green as shown to make a sashing unit. Make (4) sashing units.

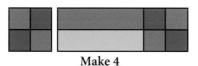

Make 4

Table Runner Assembly

1. Sew a B/C sashing unit to each side of the Pumpkin blocks as shown.

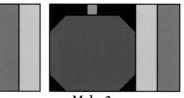

Make 2

2. Sew a B/C sashing strip unit to each side of the Thrift block as shown.

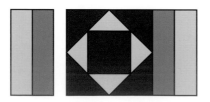

3. Referring to the Table Runner Assembly Diagram, alternate the (3) blocks with the (4) sashing rows to complete the table runner center.

4. Sew the fabric A 4-1/2" x 40-1/2" side border strips to opposite sides of the table runner center. Sew the fabric A 4-1/2" x 24-1/2" top/bottom border strips to the top/bottom of the table runner center.

Finishing the Table Runner

Layer the backing fabric, batting and table runner top. Baste the layers together. Hand or machine quilt as desired. Bind to finish the table runner.

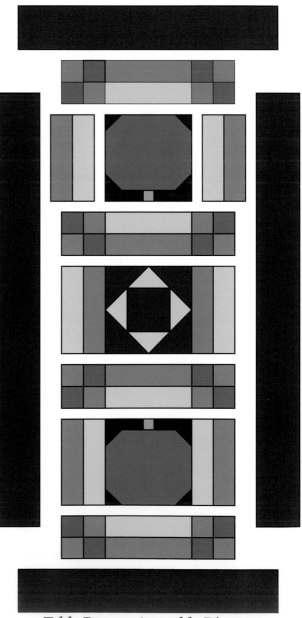

Table Runner Assembly Diagram

Winter Table Runner

The center star blocks are emphasized by the subtle stars in the sashings. A triangle added to each end of a sashing strip creates the sashing stars.

Table Runner designed and made by Jean Ann Wright.

Materials

Finished size approximately 20" x 40"

Star blocks: 8" x 8"

wof indicates width of fabric

Note: Sew all blocks with a scant 1/4" seam and press all seams as you sew.

- Fabric A—1/3 yard holly print (borders)
- Fabric B—1/4 yard tree border print (borders)
- Fabric C—1/2 yard red print (sashings)
- Fabric D—1/2 yard gold print (Star blocks, sashings)
- Fabric E—1/3 yard lime green (Star blocks, sashing squares)
- Fabric F—1 yard white mini-print (Star blocks)
- Fabric G—1/3 yard allover tree print (binding)
- Backing—1-1/2 yards
- Thread for machine quilting
- Craft size batting

Note: Sulky® 40 wt Rayon #1051 Christmas green thread and Quilter's Dream® Green batting were used in this project.

Cutting Instructions

Fabric A, cut:
(1) 8-1/2" x wof strip, from this strip cut:
  (6) 4-1/2" x 8-1/2" side border pieces.

Fabric B, fussy cut:
(1) 6-1/2" x wof strip, from this strip cut:
  (2) 8-1/2" x 6-1/2" top/bottom border pieces.
  (4) 4-1/2" x 6-1/2" top/bottom border pieces.

Fabric C, cut:
(5) 2-1/2" x wof strips, from these strips cut:
  (10) 2-1/2" x 8-1/2" sashing strips,
  (12) 2-1/2" x 4-1/2" sashing strips and
  (4) 2-1/2" x 6-1/2" sashing strips.

Fabric D, cut:
(2) 2-1/2" x wof strips, from these strips cut:
  (32) 2-1/2" squares.

(1) 4-1/2" x wof strip, from this strip cut:
  (3) 4-1/2" squares.

Fabric E, cut:
(2) 2-1/2" x wof strips, from these strips cut:
  (20) 2-1/2" squares.

Cut (2) 2-1/2" x wof strips, from these strips cut:
  (12) 2-1/2" x 4-1/2" rectangles.

Fabric F, cut:
(2) 2-1/2" x wof strips, from these strips cut:
 (24) 2-1/2" squares.

Fabric G, cut:
(4) 2-1/4" x wof strips, sew together end-to-end
 for binding.

Star Block Assembly

Note: Refer to Flying Geese directions on page 12 to construct the block.

1. Lay a fabric F 2-1/2" square on one side of a fabric E 2-1/2" x 4-1/2" rectangle, right sides together. Sew a diagonal line across the 2-1/2" square and through the fabric layers.

2. Trim 1/4" away from the sewn line and press the seam allowance toward the triangle.

3. Lay a fabric F 2-1/2" square on the opposite side of the fabric E 2-1/2" x 4-1/2" rectangle. Sew and press as before to complete a Flying Geese unit. Make (12) Flying Geese units.

Make 12

4. Sew a Flying Geese unit to opposite sides of a fabric D 4-1/2" square to make a block center. Make (3) block centers.

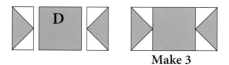

Make 3

5. Sew a fabric E 2-1/2" square to opposite sides of the remaining Flying Geese units.

Make 3

6. Lay out (2) Flying Geese units and a block center. Sew the units together to make a Star block. Make (3) Star blocks.

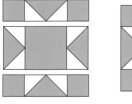

Make 3

Sashing Assembly

1. Lay a fabric D 2-1/2" square on each end of a Fabric C 2-1/2" x 8-1/2" sashing strip, right sides together. Sew in a diagonal line across the 2-1/2" square and through the fabric layers as shown. Make sure both seams are going in the same direction.

2. Trim 1/4" away from the sewn line and press seams toward the triangles to make a long C/D sashing strip. Make (10) long C/D sashing strips.

Make 10

3. Lay a fabric D 2-1/2" square on the right end of a fabric C 2-1/2" x 4-1/2" sashing strip, right sides together. Sew a diagonal line in the same direction as the long C/D sashing strips. Make (12) short C/D sashing strips. Repeat with the fabric C 2-1/2" x 6-1/2" sashing strips and the fabric D 2-1/2" squares to make (4) medium C/D sashing strips.

Make 8   Make 4

Sashing Row Assembly

Lay out (2) short C/D sashing strips, (2) fabric E 2-1/2" squares and (1) long C/D sashing strip, as shown. Check the orientation of the triangle star points. Sew the pieces together to complete a sashing row. Make (4) sashing rows.

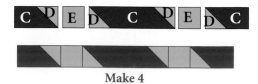

Make 4

Table Runner Assembly

1. Sew a long C/D sashing strip to each side of a Star block. Make (3).

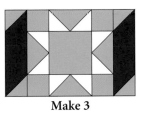

Make 3

2. Sew a fabric A 4-1/2" x 8-1/2" side border piece to the units made in step 1. Make (3).

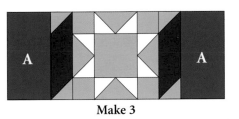

Make 3

3. Referring to the Table Runner Assembly Diagram, lay out (4) sashing rows and (3) block rows. Sew the rows together to complete the table runner center.

4. Lay out (2) fabric B 4-1/2" x 6-1/2" border pieces, (2) medium C/D sashing strips and (1) fabric B 8-1/2" x 6-1/2" border piece, as shown. Check the orientation of the triangle star points. Sew the pieces together to complete a top/bottom border. Make (2) top/bottom borders.

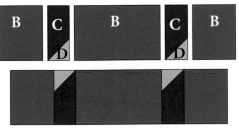

Make 2

5. Referring to the Table Runner Assembly Diagram, sew the top/bottom borders to the table runner center.

Finishing the Table Runner

Layer the backing fabric, batting and table runner top. Baste the layers together. Hand or machine quilt as desired. Bind to finish the table runner.

Table Runner Assembly Diagram

This Shoo Fly quilt is sewn together in a block to block setting. The blocks have varying background colors and prints which bring the quilt to life and make it visually exciting.

Block to Block Settings

One of the easiest and quickest ways to sew a quilt together is to simply leave out the sashings. By sewing a quilt together block to block you can create dozens of interesting settings. Use one block in different color combinations, alternate two blocks checkerboard style or create a woven type setting with three blocks.

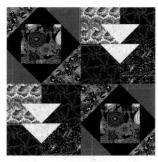

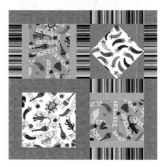

Shoo Fly Pie

The blocks in this small jewel of a quilt call out for attention. Even though the blocks are repeated and placed side by side, the placement of the fabric colors allows each to stand out on its own. Only two blocks are actually identical. For most block to block settings an inner border is added to 'stop' the design and give the eye a rest before moving to the outer border.

Quilt designed and made by Jean Ann Wright.

Materials

Finished size approximately 39" x 39"

Shoo Fly blocks: 7-1/2" x 7-1/2"

wof indicates width of fabric

Note: Sew all blocks with a scant 1/4" seam and press all seams as you sew.

- Fabric A—2/3 yard black print
  (inner and outer borders, binding)

- Fabric B—2/3 yard white with black geometric print (Shoo Fly blocks, outer borders)

- Fabric C—1/3 yard purple print
  (Shoo Fly blocks, outer borders)

- Fabric D—1/3 yard teal print
  (Shoo Fly blocks, outer borders)

- Fabric E—1/3 yard gold print
  (Shoo Fly blocks, outer borders)

- Fabric F—1/3 yard lime green texture print
  (Shoo Fly blocks, outer borders)

- Fabric G—3/4 yard fuchsia texture print
  (Shoo Fly blocks, outer borders)

- Backing—1-1/4 yards

- Thread for machine quilting

- Craft or crib size batting

Note: Sulky® 30 wt Blendables® #4119 Piano Keys thread and Quilter's Dream® Cotton batting were used in this project.

Cutting Instructions

Fabric A, cut:
(4) 2" x wof strips, from these strips cut:
  (2) 2" x 30-1/2" side inner border strips and
  (2) 2" x 33-1/2" top/bottom inner border strips.
  From leftover 2" border strips cut:
  (16) 2" squares.

(4) 2-1/4" x wof strips, sew together end-to-end for binding.

Fabric B, cut:
(4) 2" x wof strips, from these strips cut:
  (68) 2" squares.

(3) 3-7/8" x wof strips, from these strips cut:
  (24) 3-7/8" squares.

Fabric C, cut:
(3) 2" x wof strips, from these strips cut:
  (54) 2" squares.

(1) 3-7/8" x wof strip, from this strip cut:
  (8) 3-7/8" squares.

Fabric D, cut:
(3) 2" x wof strips, from these strips cut:
  (51) 2" squares.

(1) 3-7/8" x wof strip, from this strip cut:
  (8) 3-7/8" squares.

Fabric E, cut:
(3) 2" x wof strips, from these strips cut:
  (56) 2" squares.

(1) 3-7/8" x wof strip, from this strip cut:
  (8) 3-7/8" squares.

Fabric F, cut:
(3) 2" x wof strips, from these strips cut:
  (45) 2" squares.

(1) 3-7/8" x wof strip, from this strip cut:
  (8) 3-7/8" squares.

Fabric G, cut:
(3) 2" x wof strips, from these strips cut:
  (46) 2" squares.

(1) 3-7/8" x wof strip, from this strip cut:
  (8) 3-7/8" squares.

Block Assembly

Note: Refer to Half-square Triangle directions on page 9 to construct the block.

Shoo Fly blocks:

1. Draw a diagonal line from corner to corner on the wrong side of the (24) fabric B 3-7/8" squares and the (8) fabric E 3-7/8" squares.

2. Lay a marked fabric E 3-7/8" square on a fabric D 3-7/8" square, right sides together. Sew 1/4" on each side of the drawn line.

3. Cut on the drawn line and press toward the dark triangles to make (2) half-square triangle units.

4. Refer to the diagrams to make a total of (64) half-square triangle units in the color combinations shown.

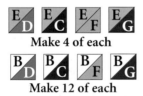

Make 4 of each

Make 12 of each

5. Sew together pairs of fabric B, C, D, E, F and G 2" squares in the color combinations shown for a total of (64) double square units.

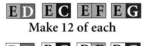

Make 12 of each

Make 4 of each

6. Referring to the Block Assembly Diagram for color placement, sew a contrasting C - G 2" square between (2) matching double square units to form a center block row. Refer to diagram in Step 8 to make (16) center block rows; each in different color combinations.

Make 16

7. Lay out (4) matching half-square triangle units, (2) matching double square units and (1) center block row. Sew the pieces together in rows and sew the rows together to make a Shoo Fly block.

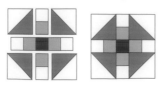

8. Make (16) Shoo Fly blocks referring to the Block Assembly Diagram for color placement.

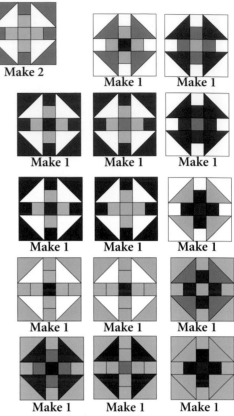

Make 2

Make 1   Make 1

Make 1   Make 1   Make 1

Make 1   Make 1   Make 1

Make 1   Make 1   Make 1

Make 1   Make 1   Make 1

Block Assembly Diagram

Four Patch blocks:

1. Layer a fabric B 2" square and a fabric F 2" square, right sides together. Sew the squares together along one side. Press squares open. Make another B/F unit in the same manner.

2. Layer the B/F units, right sides together, with the fabric B square on the fabric F square. Sew the units together and press open to make a Four Patch block.

3. Repeat steps 1 - 2 using the (16) fabric A 2" squares and the remaining fabric B - G 2" squares to make (48) Four Patch blocks in the color combinations shown.

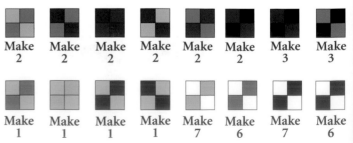

Make 2   Make 2   Make 2   Make 2   Make 2   Make 2   Make 3   Make 3

Make 1   Make 1   Make 1   Make 1   Make 7   Make 6   Make 7   Make 6

Quilt Center Assembly

Referring to the Quilt Assembly Diagram, lay out the Shoo Fly blocks in (4) rows with (4) blocks in each row. Sew the blocks together in rows and then sew the rows together to complete the quilt center.

Borders

1. Referring to the Quilt Assembly Diagram, sew the fabric A 2" x 30-1/2" side inner border strips to opposite sides of the quilt center. Sew the fabric A 2" x 33-1/2" top/bottom inner border strips to the top/bottom of the quilt center.

2. Referring to the Quilt Assembly Diagram, sew (11) Four Patch blocks together as shown to make a side outer border. Repeat to make a second side outer border. Sew the side outer borders to opposite sides of the quilt center.

3. Referring to the Quilt Assembly Diagram, sew (13) Four Patch blocks together as shown to make a top/bottom outer border. Repeat to make a second top/bottom outer border. Sew the top/bottom outer borders to the top/bottom of the quilt center.

Finishing the Quilt

Layer the backing fabric, batting and quilt top. Baste the layers together. Hand or machine quilt as desired. Bind to finish the quilt.

Quilt Assembly Diagram

Asian Allegory

The Thrift blocks and Geese in the Sky blocks are easy basic blocks set in the quilt in a bold design. Careful placement of fabric and color, as well as setting the blocks in an alternating pattern, give the quilt a fresh, appealing look. Asian Allegory would look great in any fabric palette, from vintage to modern.

Quilt designed by Janet Houts.

Materials

Finished size approximately 72" x 96"

Thrift blocks: 12" x 12"

Geese in the Sky blocks: 12" x 12"

wof indicates width of fabric

Note: Sew all blocks with a scant 1/4" seam and press all seams as you sew.

- Fabric A—2-1/8 yards Asian floral print (outer borders, binding)

- Fabric B—1 yard cream texture print (Geese in the Sky blocks, inner borders)

- Fabric C—1 yard dark brown print (Thrift blocks)

- Fabric D—1 yard medium green floral print (Thrift blocks)

- Fabric E—1 yard green bamboo texture print (Thrift blocks)

- Fabric F—2/3 yard large Asian blossom print (Thrift blocks)

- Fabric G—1 yard light green print (Geese in the Sky blocks)

- Fabric H—1 yard medium/dark rust print (Geese in the Sky blocks)

- Fabric I—1 yard dark blossom dot print (Geese in the Sky blocks)

- Backing—5-2/3 yards

- Thread for machine quilting

- Queen size batting

Note: Sulky® 30 wt Blendables® #4036 Earth Taupes thread and Quilter's Dream® Orient batting were used in this project.

Cutting Instructions

Fabric A, cut:

(9) 5-1/2" x wof strips, sew together end-to-end and cut:
    (2) 5-1/2" x 86-1/2" side outer border strips and
    (2) 5-1/2" x 72-1/2" top/bottom outer border strips.

(9) 2-1/4" x wof strips, sew together end-to-end for binding.

Fabric B, cut:

(6) 3-1/2" x wof strips, from these strips cut:
    (36) 3-1/2" x 6-1/2" rectangles.

(8) 1-1/2" x wof strips, sew together end-to-end and cut:
    (2) 1-1/2" x 72-1/2" side inner border strips and
    (2) 1-1/2" x 62-1/2" top/bottom inner border strips.

Fabric C, cut:

(4) 7-1/4" x wof strips, from these strips cut:
    (17) 7-1/4" squares; cut each square in half on the diagonal twice to make (68) quarter-square triangles.

Fabric D, cut:

(4) 6-7/8" x wof strips, from these strips cut:
    (17) 6-7/8" squares; cut each square in half on the diagonal once to make (34) half-square triangles.

Fabric E, cut:

(4) 6-7/8" x wof strips, from these strips cut:
    (17) 6-7/8" squares; cut each square in half on the diagonal once to make (34) half-square triangles.

Fabric F, cut:

(3) 6-1/2" x wof strips, from these strips cut:
    (18) 6-1/2" squares.

Fabric G, cut:

(6) 3-1/2" x wof strips, from these strips cut:
    (36) 3-1/2" squares.

(2) 3-1/2" x wof strips, from these strips cut:
    (18) 3-1/2" x 6-1/2" rectangles.

Fabric H, cut:

(6) 3-1/2" x wof strips, from these strips cut:
    (72) 3-1/2" squares.

(3) 3-1/2" x wof strips, from these strips cut:
    (36) 3-1/2" x 6-1/2" rectangles.

Fabric I, cut:

(6) 3-1/2" x wof strips, from these strips cut:
    (36) 3-1/2" squares.

(2) 3-1/2" x wof strips, from these strips cut:
    (18) 3-1/2" x 6-1/2" rectangles.

Block Assembly

Note: Refer to Flying Geese and Thrift block directions on pages 12 and 20 to construct the blocks.

Thrift blocks:

1. Lay fabric C 7-1/4" quarter-square triangles on opposite sides of a fabric F 6-1/2" square, right sides together, and sew in place. Press the seams toward the triangles. Repeat with fabric C 7-1/4" quarter-square triangles on the remaining sides. Press the seams toward the triangles to make a center unit. Make (17) center units.

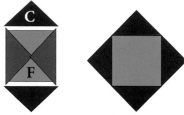

Make 17

2. Lay fabric D 6-7/8" half-square triangles on opposite sides of the center unit made in step 1, right sides together, and sew in place. Press the seams toward the triangles.

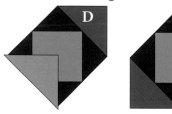

3. Lay fabric E 6-7/8" half-square triangles on the remaining sides of the center unit, right sides together. Sew in place to complete a Thrift block. Make (17) Thrift blocks.

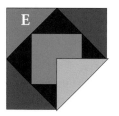

Make 17

Geese in the Sky blocks:

1. Lay a fabric G 3-1/2" square on a fabric B 3-1/2" x 6-1/2" rectangle, right sides together, as shown. Stitch in a diagonal line across the fabric G 3-1/2" square and through the fabric layers.

2. Trim 1/4" from the sewn line and press the seams toward the triangle.

3. Lay a fabric H 3-1/2" square on the opposite side of the fabric B 3-1/2" x 6-1/2" rectangle. Sew in a diagonal line across the fabric H 3-1/2" square and press the seams toward the triangle to make a G/B/H Flying Geese unit. Make (18) G/B/H Flying Geese units.

Make 18

4. Sew a fabric G 3-1/2" square to the fabric G side of the G/B/H Flying Geese unit and a fabric H 3-1/2" square to the fabric H side of the G/B/H Flying Geese unit. Make (18) extended Flying Geese units.

Make 18

5. Following steps 1 - 4, make additional Flying Geese units in the fabric H and I 3-1/2" squares on the fabric B 3-1/2" x 6-1/2" rectangles, as shown. Make (18) H/B/I units.

Make 18

6. Sew a fabric H 3-1/2" square to the fabric H side of the H/B/I Flying Geese unit and a fabric I 3-1/2" square to the fabric I side of the H/B/I Flying Geese unit. Make (18) reverse extended Flying Geese units.

7. Sew a fabric G 3-1/2" x 6-1/2" rectangle and a fabric H 3-1/2" x 6-1/2" rectangle together to make a G/H unit. Make (18) G/H units. Repeat using the fabric H and I 3-1/2" x 6-1/2" rectangles to make (18) H/I units.

Make 18   **Make 18**

8. Following the diagram shown, lay out (2) G/H units, (1) extended Flying Geese unit and (1) reverse extended Flying Geese unit in rows. Sew the rows together to complete a Geese in the Sky block. Make (18) Geese in the Sky blocks.

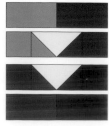

Make 18

64

Quilt Center Assembly

1. Referring to the Quilt Assembly Diagram, lay out the Geese in the Sky blocks and Thrift blocks as shown. Sew the blocks together in (7) rows with (5) blocks in each row. The odd numbered rows begin and end with a Geese in the Sky block and the even numbered rows begin and end with a Thrift block.

2. Sew the rows together to complete the quilt center.

Borders

1. Referring to the Quilt Assembly Diagram, sew the fabric B 1-1/2" x 72-1/2" side inner border strips to opposite sides of the quilt center. Sew the fabric B 1-1/2" x 62-1/2" top/bottom inner border strips to the top/bottom of the quilt center.

2. Sew the fabric A 5-1/2" x 86-1/2" side outer border strips to opposite sides of the quilt center. Sew the fabric A 5-1/2" x 72-1/2" top/bottom outer border strips to the top/bottom of the quilt top.

Finishing the Quilt

Layer the backing fabric, batting and quilt top. Baste the layers together. Hand or machine quilt as desired. Bind to finish the quilt.

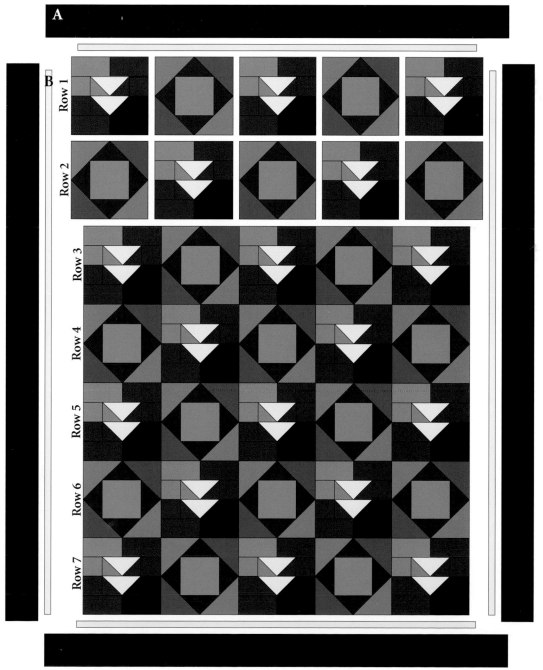

Quilt Assembly Diagram

Piñata Party

This fun quilt appears to have sashing strips, but is really three different blocks sewn together in a block to block setting. It's easy to create interesting quilt designs by setting several different blocks together. Putting the Piñata Party quilt together is a little bit like working a puzzle—the finished design only appears after the last block is stitched in place.

Quilt designed by Janet Houts.

Materials

Finished size approximately 68" x 88"

Square-in-a-Square blocks: 8" x 8"

Picture Window blocks: 12" x 12"

Rail Fence blocks: 8" x 12"

wof indicates width of fabric

Note: Sew all blocks with a scant 1/4" seam and press all seams as you sew.

- Fabric A—3/4 yard multi-color print with white background (Picture Window blocks)

- Fabric B—1 yard multi-color print with teal background (Rail Fence blocks)

- Fabric C—3/4 yard multi-color print with white background (Square-in-a-Square blocks)

- Fabric D—3/4 yard bright multi-color stripe (Rail Fence blocks)

- Fabric E—1-1/2 yards multi-color print stripe (outer borders)

- Fabric F—1-1/8 yards pink texture print (Picture Window blocks)

- Fabric G—1/2 yard bright yellow texture print (Rail Fence blocks)

- Fabric H—1-1/3 yards green texture print (inner borders)

- Fabric I—3/4 yard teal texture print (Square-in-a-Square blocks)

- Backing—5 yards

- Thread for machine quilting

- Queen size batting

Note: Sulky® 30 wt Blendables® #4041 Fiesta thread and Quilter's Dream® Cotton batting were used in this project.

Cutting Instructions

Fabric A, cut:
(3) 8-1/2" x wof strips, from these strips cut:
   (12) 8-1/2" squares.

Fabric B, cut:
(5) 6-1/2" x wof strips, from these strips cut:
   (17) 6-1/2" x 8-1/2" rectangles.

Fabric C, cut:
(3) 8-1/2" x wof strips, from these strips cut:
   (10) 8-1/2" squares.

Fabric D, cut:
(9) 2-1/2" x wof strips, from these strips cut:
   (34) 2-1/2" x 8-1/2" strips.

Fabric E, cut:
(7) 6-1/2" x wof strips, sew together end-to-end and cut:
   (2) 6-1/2" x 52-1/2" top/bottom outer border strips and
   (2) 6-1/2" x 72-1/2" side outer border strips.

Fabric F, cut:
(14) 2-1/2" x wof strips, from these strips cut:
   (24) 2-1/2" x 8-1/2" strips and
   (24) 2-1/2" x 12-1/2" strips.

Fabric G, cut:
(9) 1-1/2" x wof strips, from these strips cut:
   (34) 1-1/2" x 8-1/2" strips.

Fabric H, cut:
(7) 2-1/2" x wof strips, sew together end-to-end and cut:
   (2) 2-1/2" x 52-1/2" top/bottom inner border strips and
   (2) 2-1/2" x 72-1/2" side inner border strips.

(8) 2-1/4" x wof strips, sew together end-to-end for binding.

Fabric I, cut:
(5) 4-1/2" x wof strips, from these strips cut:
   (40) 4-1/2" squares.

Block Assembly

Note: Refer to Square-in-a-Square block directions on page 14 to make the blocks.

Square-in-a-Square blocks:
1. Draw a diagonal line from corner to corner on the wrong side of the (40) fabric I 4-1/2" squares. Lay a fabric I 4-1/2" square on opposite corners of a fabric C 8-1/2" square, right sides together. Sew on the drawn lines.

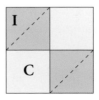

2. Trim 1/4" away from the drawn lines and press seams toward the triangles.

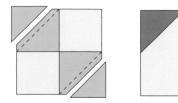

3. Repeat steps 1 - 2 in the remaining corners of the fabric C 8-1/2" square to complete the Square-in-a-Square block. Make (10) Square-in-a-Square blocks.

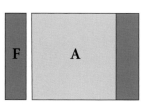

Make 10

Picture Window blocks:

1. Sew a fabric F 2-1/2" x 8-1/2" strip to opposite sides of a fabric A 8-1/2" square.

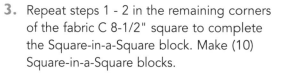

2. Sew a fabric F 2-1/2" x 12-1/2" strip to the remaining sides of the fabric A 8-1/2" square to make a Picture Window block. Make (12) Picture Window blocks.

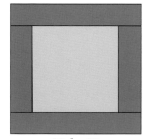

Make 12

Rail Fence blocks:

1. Sew a fabric D 2-1/2" x 8-1/2" strip and a fabric G 1-1/2" x 8-1/2" strip together to make a D/G strip set. Make (34) D/G strip sets.

2. Sew D/G strip sets to opposite sides of a fabric B 6-1/2" x 8-1/2" rectangle. Position fabric G next to the fabric B rectangles to make a Rail Fence block. Make (17) Rail Fence blocks.

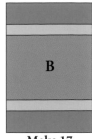

Make 17

Quilt Center Assembly

1. Referring to the Quilt Assembly Diagram, lay out the Picture Window blocks, Rail Fence blocks and Square-in-a-Square blocks as shown. Sew the blocks together in (7) rows with (5) blocks in each row. Carefully position the Rail Fence blocks to match the diagram. There will be (4) Square-in-a-Square blocks left over for the border corners.

2. Sew the rows together to complete the quilt center.

Borders

1. Sew a fabric H 2-1/2" x 52-1/2" top/bottom inner border strip and a fabric E 6-1/2" x 52-1/2" top/bottom outer border strip together to make a top/bottom border. Make (2) top/bottom borders.

2. Sew a fabric H 2-1/2" x 72-1/2" side inner border strip and a fabric E 6-1/2" x 72-1/2" side outer border strip together to make a side border. Make (2) side borders.

3. Referring to the Quilt Assembly Diagram, sew the side borders to opposite sides of the quilt center with fabric H positioned next to the quilt center.

4. Sew a Square-in-a-Square block to each end of the top/bottom borders. Sew the top/bottom borders to the top and bottom of the quilt center, with H positioned next to the quilt center.

Finishing the Quilt

Layer the backing fabric, batting and quilt top. Baste the layers together. Hand or machine quilt as desired. Bind to finish the quilt.

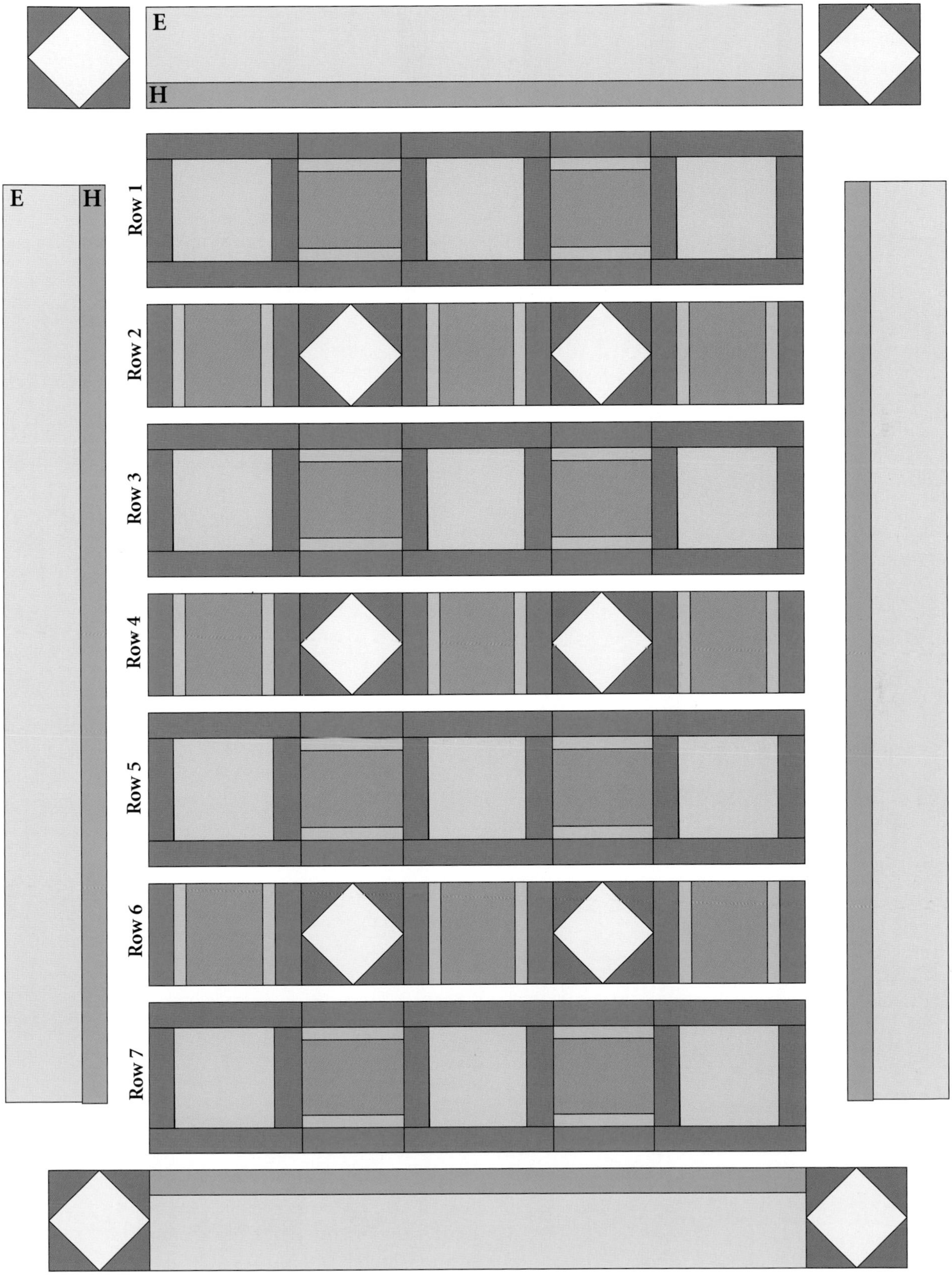

E

H

E   H

Row 1

Row 2

Row 3

Row 4

Row 5

Row 6

Row 7

Quilt Assembly Diagram

Wheel of Mystery

Repeating one block in a block to block setting doesn't need to be boring. The Wheel of Mystery quilt alternates the black and white prints within twelve of the blocks and then drops in a dash of bright color in the remaining four. The blocks are easy to appliqué and take no time at all to sew. Substituting another block in your favorite colors would give this quilt an entirely new look.

Quilt designed and made by Debby Kratovil.

Materials

Finished size approximately 56" x 56"

Appliqué blocks: 10" x 10"

wof indicates width of fabric

Note: Sew all blocks with a scant 1/4" seam and press all seams as you sew.

- Fabric A—2/3 yard white with small black/white floral print (Appliqué blocks)

- Fabric B—2/3 yard white with geometric black lines (Appliqué blocks)

- Fabric C—1-1/8 yard black with geometric black lines (Appliqué blocks, binding)

- Fabric D—2/3 yard black with flowers (Appliqué blocks)

- Fabric E—1/2 yard bright multi-color allover print (Appliqué blocks)

- Fabric F—1/4 yard multi-color stripe (inner borders)

- Fabric G—3/4 yard black with large floral print (outer borders)

- Backing—3-1/2 yards

- Template on page 72

- Freezer paper

- Fusible interfacing

- Thread for machine quilting

- Queen size batting

- Template plastic

- Temporary spray adhesive

Note: Sulky® 30 wt Blendables® #4034 Soft Blacks thread and Quilter's Dream® Orient batting were used in this project.

Cutting Instructions

Fabric A, cut:
(2) 10-1/2" x wof strips, from these strips cut:
  (8) 10-1/2" squares.

Fabric B, cut:
(2) 10-1/2" x wof strips, from these strips cut:
  (8) 10-1/2" squares.

Fabric C, cut:
(2) 10-1/2" x wof strips, from these strips cut:
  (6) 10-1/2" squares.

(6) 2-1/4" wof strips, sew together end-to-end for binding.

Fabric D, cut
(2) 10-1/2" x wof strips, from these strips cut:
  (6) 10-1/2" squares.

Fabric E, cut:
(2) 10-1/2" x wof strips, from these strips cut:
  (4) 10-1/2" squares.

Fabric F, cut:
(4) 1-1/2" x wof strips, from these strips cut:
  (2) 1-1/2" x 40-1/2" side inner border strips and
  (2) 1-1/2" x 42-1/2" top/bottom inner border strips.

Fabric G, cut:
(5) 7-1/2" x wof strips, sew together end-to-end and cut:
  (2) 7-1/2" x 42-1/2" side outer border strips and
  (2) 7-1/2" x 56-1/2" top/bottom outer border strips.

Block Assembly

1. Trace the template on page 72 onto template plastic or paper and cut out.

2. Fold a piece of 10-1/2" freezer paper into quarters. Place the fold lines of the template on the fold lines of the freezer paper. Carefully cut out a full size appliqué template. Make (16) full size appliqué templates.

3. Following manufacturer's directions, transfer the fusible interfacing to the wrong side of (4) fabric A 10-1/2" squares, (4) fabric B 10-1/2" squares, (2) fabric C 10-1/2" squares, (2) fabric D 10-1/2" squares and (4) fabric E 10-1/2" squares. Allow to cool after ironing the interfacing in place. Iron the freezer paper templates to the right sides of the fabric/interfacing squares and cut out.

4. Referring to the block diagrams below, center the appliqué shapes on the remaining 10-1/2" squares. Allow 1/4" around all edges for seam allowances. Use a temporary spray adhesive to hold the appliqués in place and use a narrow zigzag stitch to sew it to the square. Make (16) Appliqué blocks.

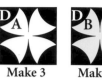
Make 3

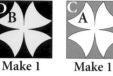
Make 1

Make 1

Make 3

Make 1

Make 1

Make 1

Make 1

Make 2

Make 2

Quilt Center Assembly

Referring to the Quilt Assembly Diagram for placement, lay out the blocks in (4) rows with (4) blocks in each row. Sew the rows together to make the quilt center.

Borders

1. Referring to the Quilt Assembly Diagram, sew the fabric F 1-1/2" x 40-1/2" side inner border strips to opposite sides of the quilt center. Sew the 1-1/2" x 42-1/2" top/bottom inner border strips to the top/bottom of the quilt center.

2. Referring to the Quilt Assembly Diagram, sew the fabric G 7-1/2" x 42-1/2" side outer border strips to opposite sides of the quilt center. Sew the 7-1/2" x 56-1/2" top/bottom outer border strips to the top/bottom of the quilt center to complete the quilt.

Finishing the Quilt

Layer the backing fabric, batting and quilt top. Baste the layers together. Hand or machine quilt as desired. Bind to finish the quilt.

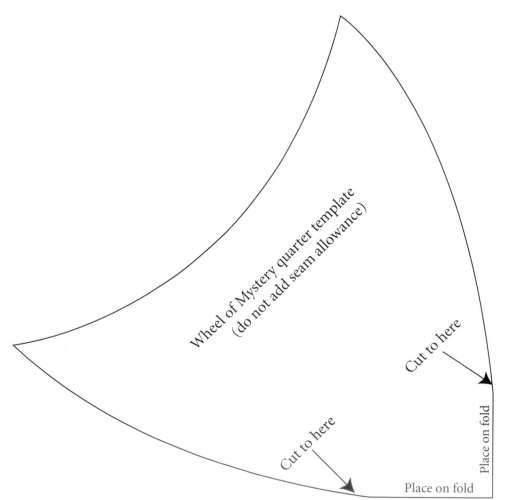

Wheel of Mystery quarter template (do not add seam allowance)

Cut to here

Cut to here

Place on fold

Place on fold

Full-size template

Quilt Assembly Diagram

*This little charmer has the overall appearance of stars placed in a
woven field of Rail Fence blocks. The trick is to carefully watch the
orientation of the blocks as you sew each individual row together. The stars,
in contrast, are sewn in willy-nilly to add a whimsical appearance to the finished quilt.*

Diagonal Settings

Diagonal settings bring energy and excitement to a quilt. They can seem a little intimidating at first sight, but if sewn together in steps they are easy to assemble. The key is to arrange your blocks on a flannel design wall or spare bed and then sew the diagonal rows together one at a time. When each row is finished, place it back in the quilt block arrangement before starting the next row. The rows will then be ready to be sewn together with little effort.

For more information on setting blocks on the diagonal, see page 23.

Stars and Bars

A block to block setting can also be used in a diagonal set quilt. In Stars and Bars, Rail Fence and Star Appliqué blocks are alternated and then sewn together in diagonal rows. The difference between a straight block to block setting and a diagonal block to block setting is the addition of setting and corner triangles in the diagonally set quilt top.

Quilt designed and made by Jean Ann Wright.

Materials

Finished size approximately 27" x 31"

Rail Fence blocks: 3" x 3"

Star Appliqué blocks: 3" x 3"

wof indicates width of fabric

Note: Sew all blocks with a scant 1/4" seam and press all seams as you sew.

- Fabric A—1/2 yard dark green print (inner borders, binding)

- Fabric B—1/2 yard solid cream (Star Appliqué blocks, setting triangles)

- Fabric C—1/2 yard cream small print (Rail Fence blocks, Nine Patch outer border blocks)

- Fat Quarters—(12) jewel tone allover prints (Star Appliqué blocks, Rail Fence blocks, Nine Patch blocks)

- Backing—1 yard

- Thread for machine quilting

- Craft size batting

- Fusible web for appliqué

Note: Sulky® 30 wt Blendables® #4001 Parchment thread and Quilter's Dream® Green batting were used in this project.

Note:

In sewing many small pieces together the number of units required to make a border strip does not always come out even. I added one extra unit to the left side border, two side units to the right side border and 1 extra unit to the bottom border to make the borders fit evenly. These extra units may not always be needed.

Cutting Instructions

Fabric A, cut:

(4) 1-1/2" x wof inner border strips.

(4) 2-1/4" x wof strips, sew together end-to-end for binding.

Fabric B, cut

(1) 5-1/2" x wof strip, from this strip cut:
(5) 5-1/2" squares; cut each square in half on the diagonal twice to make (20) quarter-square triangles. (2) will be extra.
Trim the remainder of this strip to 3", from this strip cut:
(2) 3" squares; cut the squares on the diagonal once to make (4) half-square triangles.

(2) 3-1/2" x wof strips, from these strips cut:
(20) 3-1/2" squares.

Fabric C, cut:

(3) 1-1/2" x wof strips, from these strips cut:
(30) 1-1/2" x 3-1/2" rectangles.

(6) 1-1/2" x wof strips, from these strips cut:
(157) 1-1/2" squares.

Fat Quarters, cut:

(1) 3" square from (6) of the fat quarters.

(2) 3" squares from (6) of the fat quarters.

From the remainder of each fat quarter cut:
1-1/2" x wof strips, from each strip cut:
(5) 1-1/2" x 3-1/2" rectangles.
From the remainder of each strip cut: 1-1/2" squares for a total of (159) 1-1/2" squares.

Block Assembly

Star Appliqué blocks:

Trace (20) star templates from the pattern on page 79 onto fusible web. Cut the templates out on the drawn lines. Following manufacturer's directions, adhere the fused templates to the jewel tone 3" squares. Cut out the star appliqués. Center each of the star appliqués on a fabric B 3-1/2" square and fuse in place. Stitch the star appliqués in place using your favorite machine appliqué method. Make (20) Star Appliqué blocks.

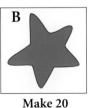

Make 20

Rail Fence blocks:

Sew jewel tone 1-1/2" x 3-1/2" rectangles to opposite sides of a fabric C 1-1/2" x 3-1/2" rectangle to make a Rail Fence block. Make (30) Rail Fence blocks.

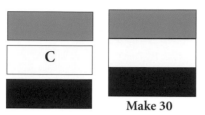

Make 30

Nine Patch blocks:

1. Lay out (5) jewel tone 1-1/2" squares and (4) fabric C 1-1/2" squares, as shown. Sew the squares together to make a Nine Patch block A. Using a variety of jewel tone 1-1/2" squares and fabric C 1-1/2" squares, make (16) Nine Patch block A.

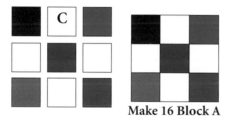

Make 16 Block A

2. Lay out (4) jewel tone 1-1/2" squares and (5) fabric C 1-1/2" squares, as shown. Sew the squares together to make a Nine Patch block B. Using a variety of jewel tone 1-1/2" squares and fabric C 1-1/2" squares, make (18) Nine Patch block B.

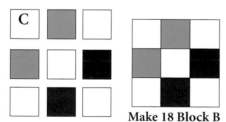

Make 18 Block B

3. Using the remaining jewel tone 1-1/2" squares and fabric C 1-1/2" squares, make (3) end border pieces and (1) alternate end border piece as shown.

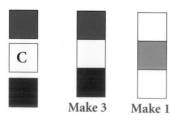

Make 3   **Make 1**

Quilt Center Assembly

1. Sew a fabric B 5-1/2" quarter-square triangle to each side of a Rail Fence block and press seams toward triangles. Sew a fabric B 3" half-square triangle to the top of the Rail Fence block to make a corner unit. Make (2) corner units alternating the orientation of the Rail Fence block in each.

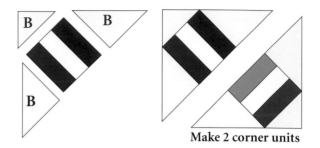

Make 2 corner units

2. Referring to the Quilt Assembly Diagram, lay out the remaining (28) Rail Fence blocks, (20) Star Appliqué blocks, (14) fabric B 5-1/2" quarter-square triangles and (2) fabric B half-square triangles as shown, carefully watching the orientation of the Rail Fence blocks in each of the rows. Sew the pieces together in diagonal rows to make the quilt center.

3. Sew the (2) corner units to the quilt center.

Borders

1. Referring to the Quilt Assembly Diagram, sew (2) fabric A 1-1/2" x wof inner border strips to opposite sides of the quilt center. Trim the quilt center to 21-1/2" from side to side.

2. Sew (2) fabric A 1-1/2" x wof inner border strips to the quilt center. Trim the quilt center to 25-1/2" from top to bottom. Note: Trimming after the borders are added on a diagonal setting allows the border width size to be flexible and accommodate the pieced Nine Patch borders.

3. Referring to the Quilt Assembly Diagram, alternate (4) Nine Patch A blocks and (4) Nine Patch B blocks to form a checkerboard pattern for the side outer borders. Make (2) side outer borders. Sew (1) end border piece to each side outer border as shown. Sew the borders to the quilt center.

4. Referring to the Quilt Assembly Diagram, alternate (4) Nine Patch A blocks and (5) Nine Patch B blocks to form a checkerboard pattern for the top/bottom outer border. Make (2) top/bottom outer borders and sew to the quilt center.

Finishing the Quilt

Layer the backing fabric, batting and quilt top. Baste
the layers together. Hand or machine quilt as desired.
Bind to finish the quilt.

**Star Appliqué
Template**

Template shape has been reversed for you.

*Note: Not all fusible web products require the
pattern to be reversed. Check the manufacturer's
instructions before beginning.*

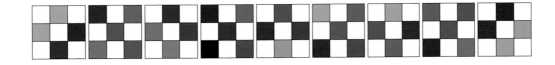

Quilt Assembly Diagram

79

Churn Dash

Don't shy away from bright, fun prints when creating diagonal set quilts. I used large scale prints in the setting blocks and the side setting and corner triangles. All the fabrics used in the diagonal set Churn Dash quilt come together to give it a feeling of whimsy and motion.

Quilt designed and made by Jean Ann Wright.

Materials

Finished size approximately 54" x 68-1/2"

Churn Dash blocks: 10" x 10"

wof indicates width of fabric

Note: Sew all blocks with a scant 1/4" seam and press all seams as you sew.

- Fabric A—2 yards large print (setting squares, setting and corner triangles, border cornerstones)

- Fabric B—1 yard stripe (outer borders)

- Fabric C—1 yard light olive green small print (inner borders, binding)

- Fabric D—1 yard cream with large polka dot print (Churn Dash blocks)

- Fabrics E-J—1 fat quarter each of purple, violet, teal, green, orange and gold

- Backing— 4 yards

- Thread for machine quilting

- Twin size batting

Note: Sulky® 30 wt Blendables® #4026 Earth Pastels thread and Quilter's Dream® Cotton batting were used in this quilt.

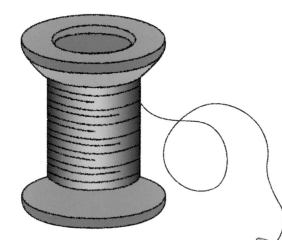

Cutting Instructions

Fabric A, cut:

(2) 10-1/2" x wof strips, from these strips cut:
    (6) 10-1/2" setting squares.

(2) 15-3/8" x wof strips, from these strips cut:
    (3) 15-3/8" squares; cut each square in half on the diagonal twice to make (12) setting triangles; (2) will be extra.

(1) 8" x wof strip, from this strip cut:
    (2) 8" squares; cut each square in half on the diagonal once to make (4) corner triangles. Trim the remainder of the strip to 4-1/2" and cut:
    (4) 4-1/2" border cornerstones.

Fabric B, cut:

(7) 4-1/2" x wof strips, sew together end-to-end and cut:
    (2) 4-1/2" x 61" side outer border strips and
    (2) 4-1/2" x 47" top/bottom outer border strips.

Fabric C, cut:

(5) 2-1/2" x wof strips, sew together end-to-end and cut:
    (2) 2-1/2" x 57" side inner border strips and
    (2) 2-1/2" x 47" top/bottom inner border strips.

(7) 2-1/4" x wof strips, sew together end-to-end for binding.

Fabric D, cut:

(3) 4-7/8" x wof strips, from these strips cut:
    (24) 4-7/8" squares.

(4) 2-1/2" x wof strips, cut: (3) strips in half to make
    (6) 2-1/2" x 22" strips. Cut the remaining strip into
    (12) 2-1/2" squares.

Fabrics E-J—Across the 22" width of each fat quarter, cut:

(1) 4-7/8" x width of fat quarter strip, from this strip cut:
    (4) 4-7/8" squares.

(1) 2-1/2" x 22" strip.

Block Assembly

Note: Refer to Half-square Triangle directions on page 9 to construct the block.

Churn Dash blocks:

1. Draw a diagonal line from corner to corner on the wrong side of the (24) fabric D 4-7/8" squares.

2. Lay a marked fabric D 4-7/8" square on a fabric E 4-7/8" square, right sides together. Sew 1/4" on each side of the drawn line.

3. Cut on the drawn line and press toward the dark triangle to make (2) half-square triangle units.

4. Using the remaining fabric D 4-7/8" squares and the fabric E - J 4-7/8" squares, make (8) half-square triangle units in each color for a total of (48) half-square triangle units.

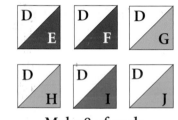

Make 8 of each

5. Lay a fabric D 2-1/2" x 22" strip on the fabric E 2-1/2" x 22" strip, right sides together. Sew the strips together along one long edge. Press seam allowances toward the darker fabric to make a strip set. Crosscut the strip set at 2-1/2" intervals to make (8) two patch units.

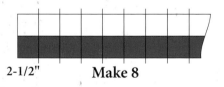

2-1/2" **Make 8**

6. Using the remaining fabric D 2-1/2" x 22" strips and the fabric F - J 2-1/2" x 22" strips, make (8) two patch units in each color combination for a total of (48) two patch units.

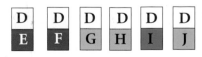
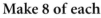

Make 8 of each

7. Referring to the Block Assembly Diagram, lay out (4) matching half-square triangle units, (4) matching two patch units and (1) fabric D 2-1/2" square. Sew the pieces together in rows and sew the rows together to make a Churn Dash block. Make (2) Churn Dash blocks in each color for a total of (12) Churn Dash blocks.

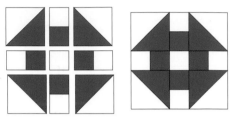

Block Assembly Diagram

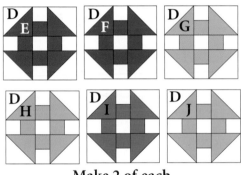

Make 2 of each

Quilt Center Assembly

1. Referring to the Quilt Assembly Diagram, lay out the (12) Churn Dash blocks, the (6) fabric A 10-1/2" setting squares and the (10) fabric A 15-3/8" setting triangles as shown. Sew the pieces together in diagonal rows to make the quilt center. Watch the orientation of the triangles carefully as you sew the rows together.

2. Sew the (4) fabric A 8" corner triangles to the corners of the quilt center.

Borders

1. Referring to the Quilt Assembly Diagram, sew the fabric C 2-1/2" x 57" side inner border strips to opposite sides of the quilt center. Sew the fabric C 2-1/2" x 47" top/bottom inner border strips to the top/bottom of the quilt center.

82

2. Referring to the Quilt Assembly Diagram, sew the fabric B 4-1/2" x 61" side outer border strips to opposite sides of the quilt center. Sew a fabric A 4-1/2" border cornerstone to each side of a fabric B 4-1/2" x 47" top/bottom outer border strip. Sew these borders to the top/bottom of the quilt center to complete the quilt.

Finishing the Quilt

Layer the backing fabric, batting and quilt top. Baste the layers together. Hand or machine quilt as desired. Bind to finish the quilt.

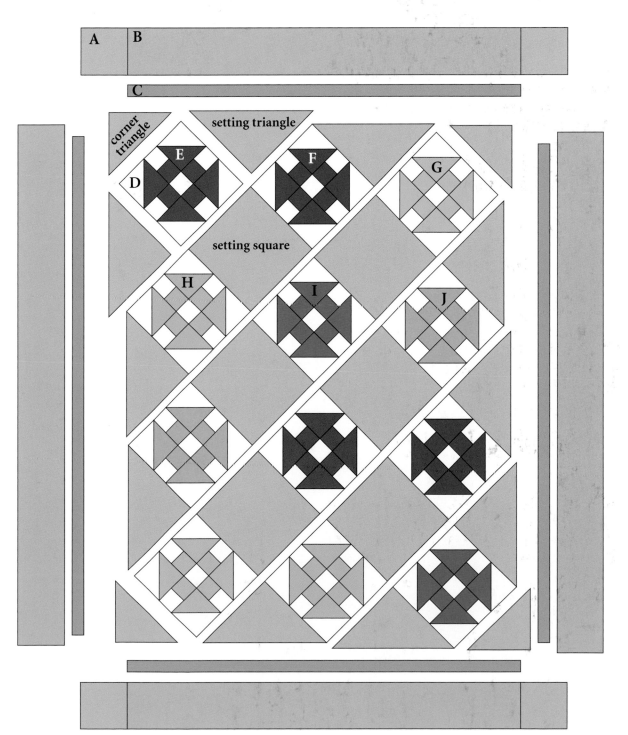

Quilt Assembly Diagram

Folk Art Posy

The posies in this quilt appear to be framed by strips of fabric. In reality, the strips are pieced Rail Fence sashing blocks alternated with Posy Appliqué blocks and sewn together in diagonal rows to make the quilt center. To square up the quilt center corner units are added to the diagonal rows. Any appliqué or traditional block can be used, making this a design you will use again and again.

Quilt designed and made by Jean Ann Wright; longarm quilting by Shannon Baker.

Posy Appliqué blocks were inspired by cameo print by Kim Schaefer for Andover Fabrics.

Materials

Finished size approximately 67-1/2" x 67-1/2"

Posy Appliqué blocks: 10" x 10"

Rail Fence sashing blocks: 6" x 10"

wof indicates width of fabric

wofq indicates 22" width of fat quarter

Note: Sew all blocks with a scant 1/4" seam and press all seams as you sew.

- Fabric A—1-1/2 yards posy or plaid print (borders)

- Fabric B—2-1/4 yards muslin or cream texture print (Posy Appliqué blocks, Rail Fence sashing blocks, setting triangles)

- Fat eighth—dark brown texture print (Posy Appliqué blocks). This fabric will be used for the posy and ladybug appliqués.

- Fat Quarters—(12) variety of plaid, floral and dot prints (Posy Appliqué blocks, Rail Fence sashing blocks). The remainder of the fat quarters will be used for the posy, stem, leaf, flower pot and ladybug appliqués.

- Backing—4 yards

- Thread for machine quilting

- Double size batting

- Fusible web for appliqué

Note: Sulky® 30 wt cotton #1022 cream thread and Quilter's Dream® Cotton batting were used in this project.

Cutting Instructions

Fabric A, cut:

(7) 6-1/2" x wof strips, sew together end-to-end and cut:
   (2) 6-1/2" x 57" side border strips and
   (2) 6-1/2" x 70" top/bottom border strips.

Fabric B, cut:

(2) 10-1/2" x wof strips, from these strips cut:
   (8) 10-1/2" squares.

(1) 15-3/8" x wof strip, from this strip cut:
   (2) 15-3/8" squares; cut each square in half on the diagonal twice to make (8) quarter-square triangles.

(2) 6-1/2" x wof strips, from these strips cut:
   (8) 6-1/2" squares. From remainder of the strip cut:
   (1) 5-1/8" square; cut the square in half on the diagonal once to make (2) half-square triangles.

(1) 9-3/4" x wof strip, from this strip cut:
   (2) 9-3/4" squares; cut each square in half on the diagonal twice to make (8) quarter-square triangles. Trim the remainder of the strip to 8" and cut:
   (1) 8" square; cut the square in half on the diagonal once to make (2) half-square triangles.

(7) 2-1/2" x wof strips, from these strips cut:
   (25) 2-1/2" x 10-1/2" strips.

Fat Quarters, cut:

(2) 2-1/2" x wof strips from each fat quarter, from these strips cut:
   (4) 2-1/2" x 10-1/2" strips.

(1) 2-1/2" x wof strip from one fat quarter, from this strip cut:
   (2) 2-1/2" x 10-1/2" strips.

85

Block Assembly
Posy Appliqué blocks:

1. Trace the templates on pages 88 - 91 onto the paper side of the fusible web and cut out. Following manufacturer's directions, adhere the appliqué shapes to the wrong side of the remaining fat quarter and fat eighth fabrics. Refer to the Quilt Assembly Diagram as a color guide if you wish. *Note: Not all fusible web products require the pattern to be reversed. Check the manufacturer's instructions before beginning.*

2. Referring to the Quilt Assembly Diagram for appliqué placement, lay out a posy, stem, leaf and flower pot appliqué shape diagonally on a fabric B 10-1/2" background square. Stitch the appliqué shapes in place using your favorite machine stitching method to make a Posy Appliqué block. Make (8) Posy Appliqué blocks adding the ladybug to one of the blocks.

Make 8

Rail Fence sashing blocks:

Sew a fat quarter 2-1/2" x 10-1/2" strip to each side of a fabric B 2-1/2" x 10-1/2" strip as shown. Press seams toward the outer strips to make a Rail Fence sashing block. Make (25) Rail Fence sashing blocks.

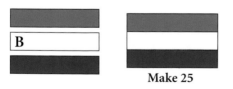

Make 25

Quilt Center Assembly

1. Lay out (1) fabric B 8" half-square triangle, (1) Rail Fence sashing block and (2) fabric B 9-3/4" quarter-square triangles as shown. Sew the pieces together to make a corner unit. Make (2) corner units.

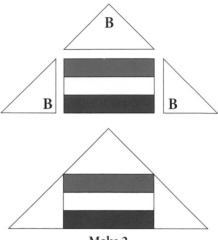

Make 2

2. Referring to the Quilt Assembly Diagram for placement, lay out (8) fabric B 15-3/8" quarter-square triangles, (8) Posy Appliqué blocks and (12) Rail Fence sashing blocks diagonally to create rows 1, 3, 5 and 7. Sew the pieces together to make the odd numbered rows.

3. Referring to the Quilt Assembly Diagram for placement, lay out (4) fabric B 9-3/4" quarter-square triangles, (8) fabric B 6-1/2" squares, (2) fabric B 5-1/8" half-square triangles and (11) Rail Fence sashing blocks diagonally to create rows 2, 4 and 6. Sew the pieces together to make the even numbered rows.

4. To assemble the quilt center, begin by sewing the pieces in row one together. Sew row one and the left corner unit together. Sew each row together in order and join it immediately to the previous row to make it easier to keep the rows in order as you sew the quilt center.

Border

1. Referring to the Quilt Assembly Diagram, sew the fabric A 6-1/2" x 57" side border strips to opposite sides of the quilt center. Trim the ends if necessary to fit the quilt center.

2. Sew the fabric A 6-1/2" x 70" top/bottom border strips to the top/bottom of the quilt center. Trim the ends if necessary to fit the quilt center.

Finishing the Quilt

Layer the backing fabric, batting and quilt top.
Baste the layers together. Hand or machine quilt as
desired. Bind to finish the quilt.

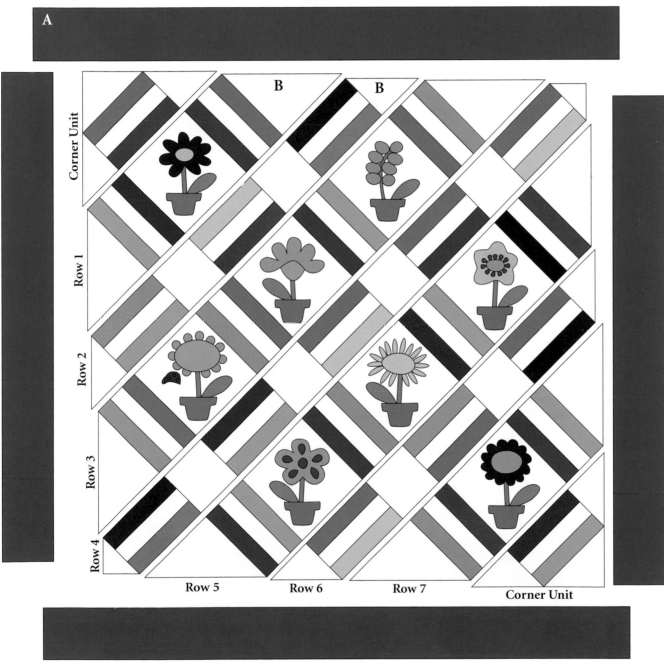

Quilt Assembly Diagram

Flower
Stems

Cut 8

Cut 1

Posy One

Cut 1

Flower Pot

Cut 8

Posy Two

Cut 1 of each shape

Leaf

Cut 4 and 4 reversed

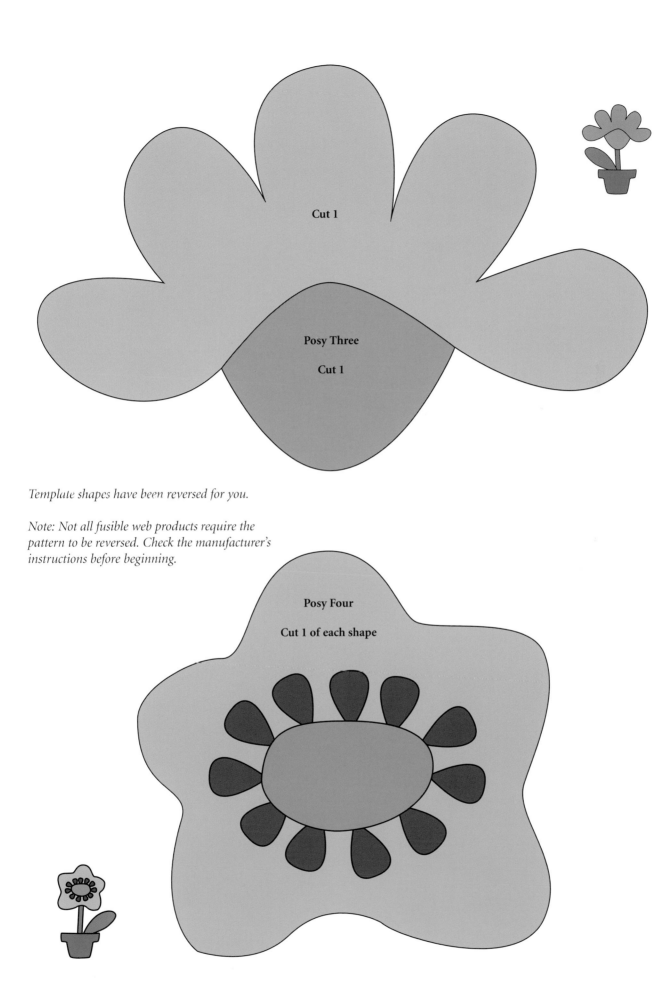

Cut 1

Posy Three

Cut 1

Template shapes have been reversed for you.

Note: Not all fusible web products require the pattern to be reversed. Check the manufacturer's instructions before beginning.

Posy Four

Cut 1 of each shape

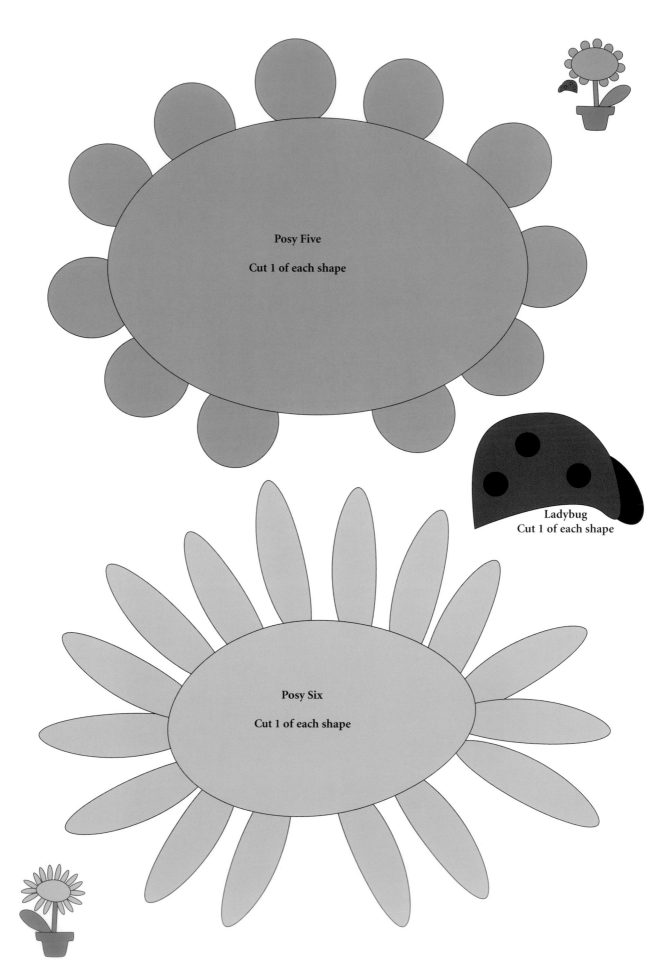

Posy Five

Cut 1 of each shape

Ladybug
Cut 1 of each shape

Posy Six

Cut 1 of each shape

Template shapes have been reversed for you.

Note: Not all fusible web products require the pattern to be reversed. Check the manufacturer's instructions before beginning.

Posy Seven

Cut 1 of each shape

Posy Eight

Cut 1 of each shape

Monkey Business

Look closely at the Monkey Business quilt. Corner triangles frame the Monkey Wrench blocks and put them "on point". Even though the quilt appears to be diagonally set it is actually sewn together in horizontal rows. Any quilt can be set "on point" with the addition of corner triangles to your favorite block. I call it my "faux" diagonal setting technique.

Quilt designed and made by Jean Ann Wright.

Materials

Finished size approximately 41" x 55"

Framed Monkey Wrench blocks: 10"

wof indicates width of fabric

Note: Sew all blocks with a scant 1/4" seam and press all seams as you sew.

- Fabric A—1-1/2 yards teal monkey print (Monkey Wrench blocks, borders)

- Fabric B—1/2 yard cream with lime green print (Monkey Wrench blocks)

- Fabric C—2/3 yard lime green geometric print (Monkey Wrench blocks, binding)

- Fabric D—1/2 yard mint green scribble print (Framed Monkey Wrench blocks)

- Fabric E—1/2 yard teal woven paisley print (Framed Monkey Wrench blocks)

- Backing—3 yards

- Thread for machine quilting

- Twin size batting

Note: Sulky® 30 wt Blendables® #4120 Springtime thread and Quilter's Dream® Cotton batting was used in this project.

Cutting Instructions

Fabric A, cut:

(4) 6-1/2" x length of fabric strips, from these strips cut:
  (2) 6-1/2" x 43" side border strips and
  (2) 6-1/2" x 41" top/bottom border strips.

(2) 4-7/8" x length of fabric strips, from these strips cut:
  (12) 4-7/8" squares.

Trim the remainder of one strip to 2-1/2", from this strip cut:
  (6) 2-1/2" squares.

Fabric B, cut:

(2) 4-7/8" x wof strips, from these strips cut:
  (12) 4-7/8" squares.

(2) 2-1/2" x wof strips.

Fabric C, cut:

(2) 2-1/2" x wof strips.

(6) 2-1/4" x wof strips, sew together end-to-end for binding.

Fabric D, cut:

(2) 8" x wof strips, from these strips cut:
  (6) 8" squares; cut each square in half on the diagonal once to make (12) half-square triangles.

Fabric E, cut:

(2) 8" x wof strips, from these strips cut:
  (6) 8" squares; cut each square in half on the diagonal once to make (12) half-square triangles.

Block Assembly

Note: Refer to Half-square Triangle directions on page 9 to construct the block.

Framed Monkey Wrench blocks:

1. Draw a diagonal line from corner to corner on the wrong side of all the fabric B 4-7/8" squares.

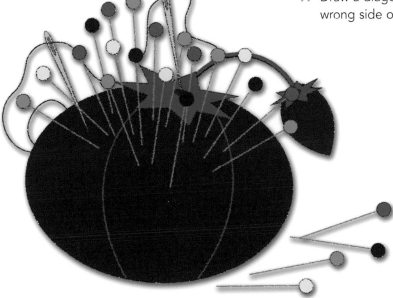

93

2. Lay a fabric B 4-7/8" square on a fabric A 4-7/8" square, right sides together. Stitch 1/4" on each side of the drawn line.

3. Cut in half on the drawn line and press seams toward dark triangle to make (2) Half-square Triangle units. Using the remaining fabric A and fabric B 4-7/8" squares, make a total of (24) half-square triangle units.

Make 24

4. Lay a fabric B 2-1/2" x wof strip on a fabric C 2-1/2" x wof strip, right sides together. Sew the strips together along one long edge. Press seam allowances toward the darker fabric to make a strip set. Crosscut the strip set at 2-1/2" intervals to make (12) B/C units. Repeat with the remaining fabric B and fabric C 2-1/2" x wof strips. Make a total of (24) B/C units.

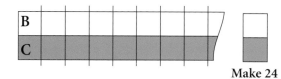

Make 24

5. Referring to the Block Assembly Diagram, lay out (4) half-square triangle units, (4) B/C units and (1) fabric A 2-1/2" square. Sew the pieces together in rows and sew the rows together to make a Monkey Wrench block. Make (6) Monkey Wrench blocks.

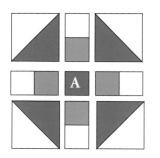
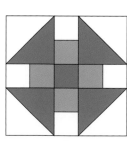

Make 6

6. Sew a fabric D 8" half-square triangle to opposite sides of a Monkey Wrench block. Press seams toward the triangles.

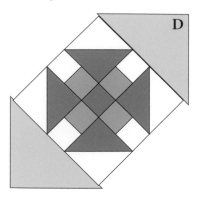

7. Sew a fabric E 8" half-square triangle to the remaining two sides of the Monkey Wrench block. Press seams toward the triangles to make a Framed Monkey Wrench block. Make (6) Framed Monkey Wrench blocks.

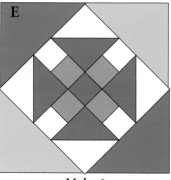

Make 6

Quilt Center Assembly

Referring to the Quilt Assembly Diagram, lay out the blocks in (3) rows with (2) blocks in each row. Sew the rows together to make the quilt center.

Borders

Referring to the Quilt Assembly Diagram, sew the fabric A 6-1/2" x 43" side border strips to opposite sides of the quilt center. Sew the fabric A 6-1/2" x 41" top/bottom border strips to the top/bottom of the quilt center.

Finishing the Quilt

Layer the backing fabric, batting and quilt top. Baste the layers together. Hand or machine quilt as desired. Bind to finish the quilt.

Quilt Assembly Diagram

Pansy Parade

Blocks set "on point" bring an appealing sense of motion to a quilt. Pansy Parade, with its diagonal setting and sashings, can be a little tricky to sew together, but if you follow the directions carefully and refer to the assembly diagram you will find the quilt comes together with ease. The finished quilt is well worth the effort and you will find yourself using this setting over and over again.

Quilt designed and made by Jean Ann Wright.

Materials

Finished size approximately 59" x 74"

Album X blocks: 8" x 8"

wof indicates width of fabric

Note: Sew all blocks with a scant 1/4" seam and press all seams as you sew.

- Fabric A—2-1/4 yards black pansy print
  (Album X blocks, sashings, outer borders)

- Fabric B—1 yard light green print
  (setting triangles)

- Fabric C—1 yard cream texture print
  (Album X blocks, sashings)

- Fabric D—1/2 yard lime green print
  (Album X blocks, inner borders)

- Fabric E—2/3 yard light purple allover print
  (Album X blocks, binding)

- 1/8 yard each of 16 bright allover prints
  (Album X blocks)

- Backing—5 yards

- Thread for machine quilting

- Twin size batting

Note: Sulky® 30 wt Blendables® #4026 Earth Pastels thread and Quilter's Dream® Orient batting were used in this project.

Cutting Instructions

Fabric A, cut:

(6) 6-1/2" x wof strips, sew together end-to-end and cut:
  (2) 6-1/2" x 62-1/2" side outer border strips and
  (2) 6-1/2" x 60-1/2" top/bottom outer border strips.

(5) 2-1/4" x wof strips, from these strips cut:
  (48) 2-1/4" x 8-1/2" sashing strips.

(2) 2-3/4" x wof strips, from these strips cut:
  (18) 2-3/4" squares.

Fabric B, cut:

(2) 15-1/4" x wof strips, from these strips cut:
  (3) 15-1/4" squares; cut each square in half on the diagonal twice to make (12) quarter-square triangles; (2) will be extra.

(2) 9-1/4" squares; cut each square in half on the diagonal once to make (4) half-square triangles.

Fabric C, cut:

(3) 6-1/4" x wof strips, from these strips cut:
  (18) 6-1/4" squares; cut each square in half on the diagonal twice to make (72) quarter-square triangles.

(2) 2-1/4" x wof strips, from these strips cut:
  (31) 2-1/4" squares.

Fabric D, cut:

(6) 2" x wof strips, from these strips cut:
  (2) 2" x 59-1/2" side inner border strips and
  (2) 2" x 48-1/2" top/bottom inner border strips.

(1) 2-3/4" x wof strip, from this strip cut:
  (4) 2-3/4" x 5-1/2" rectangles.

Fabric E, cut:

(1) 2-3/4" x wof strip, from this strip cut:
  (4) 2-3/4" x 5-1/2" rectangles.

(8) 2-1/4" wof strips, sew together end-to-end for binding.

Bright allover prints, cut:

(1) 2-3/4" x wof strip from each of the 16 fabrics, from each of these strips cut:
  (4) 2-3/4" x 5-1/2" rectangles.

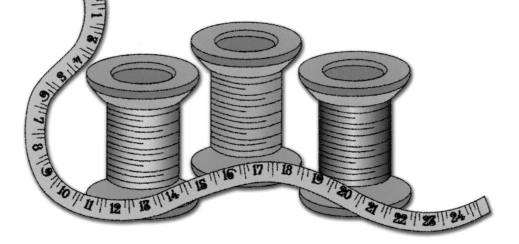

Block Assembly

Note: Refer to Album X block directions on page 21 to construct the block.

Album X blocks:

1. Sew matching fabric E 2-3/4" x 5-1/2" rectangles to each side of a fabric A 2-3/4" square. Press the seams toward the fabric A square to make the block center strip.

Make 1

2. Sew a fabric C 6-1/4" quarter-square triangle to each side of a fabric E 2-3/4" x 5-1/2" rectangle, as shown, to make a block side unit. Make (2) block side units.

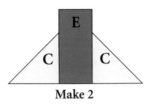

Make 2

3. Sew the block side units to each side of the center strip to make an Album X block.

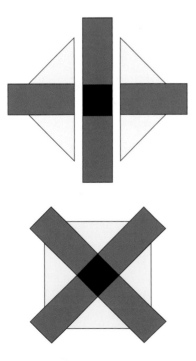

4. Referring to the Quilt Assembly Diagram, use the remaining fabric A 2-3/4" squares, the fabric D 2-3/4" x 5-1/2" rectangles, the (64) bright print 2-3/4" x 5-1/2" rectangles and the fabric C 6-1/4" quarter-square triangles to make a total of (18) Album X blocks.

5. Lay an 8-1/2" square ruler over the block with the center lines of the ruler criss-crossing the seam intersections of the center square. Trim away the excess fabric. Trim all (18) blocks.

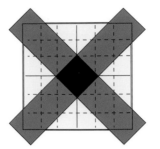

Make 18 assorted
Album X blocks

Quilt Center Assembly

1. Referring carefully to the Quilt Center Assembly Diagram for placement, lay out the Album X blocks, the fabric A 2-1/4" x 8-1/2" sashing strips, the fabric C 2-1/4" squares and the fabric B 15-1/4" quarter-square triangles in diagonal rows. Sew the pieces together in rows. You will have (6) block rows with sashings sewn in place, as shown, and (1) sashing row.

2. Sew rows 1, 2 and 3 together to complete the top half of the quilt center. Sew rows 4, 5 and 6 together to complete the bottom half of the quilt center.

3. Sew the sashing row to the top half of the quilt center and then sew the bottom half of the quilt center to this piece. Sew a fabric B 9-1/4" half-square triangle to each corner of the quilt center.

Borders

1. Sew the fabric D 2" x 59-1/2" side inner border strips to opposite sides of the quilt center. Sew the fabric D 2" x 48-1/2" top/bottom inner border strips to the top/bottom of the quilt center.

2. Sew the fabric A 6-1/2" x 62-1/2" side outer border strips to opposite sides of the quilt center. Sew the fabric A 6-1/2" x 60-1/2" top/bottom outer borders to the top/bottom of the quilt.

Finishing the Quilt

Layer the backing fabric, batting and quilt top. Baste the layers together. Hand or machine quilt as desired. Bind to finish the quilt.

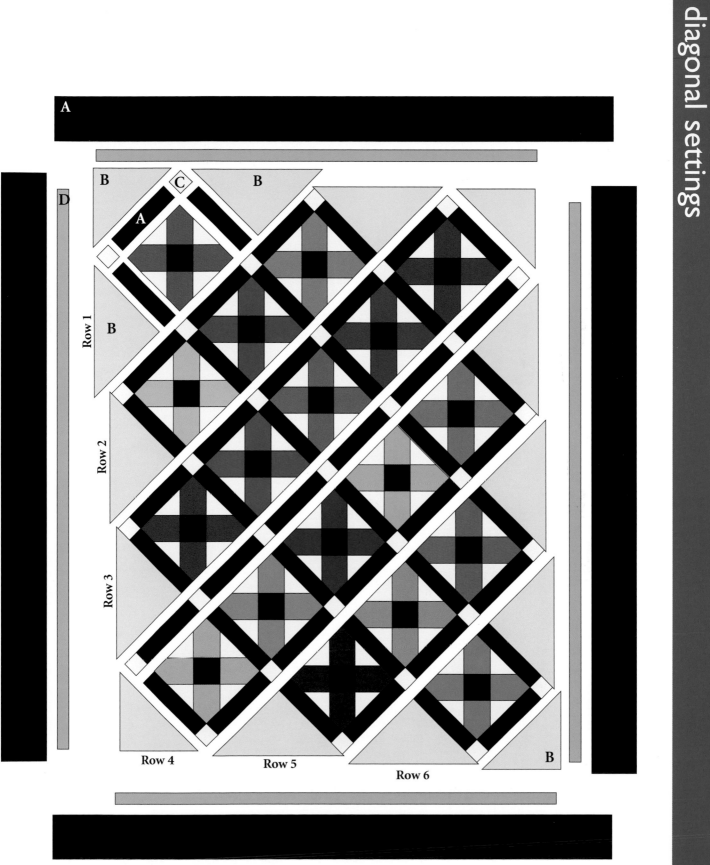

Quilt Assembly Diagram

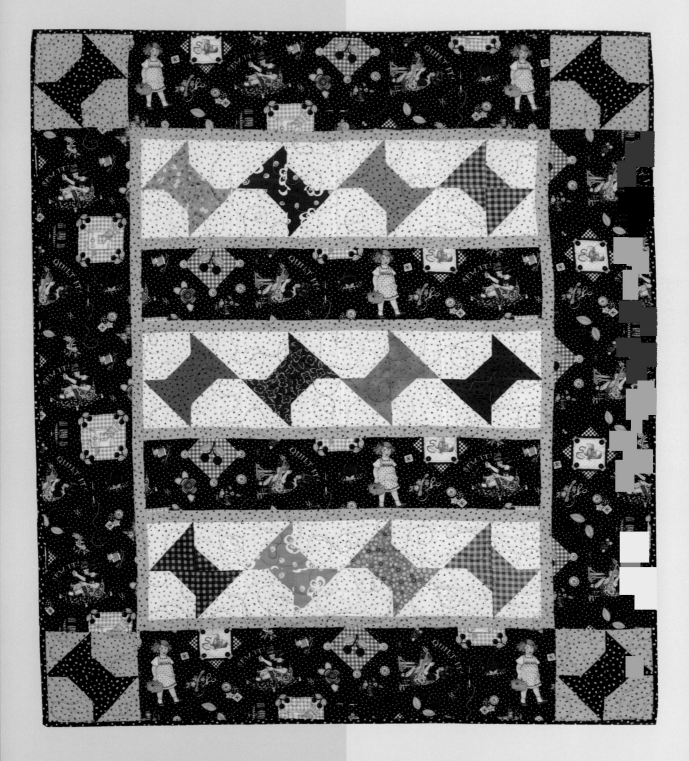

The most common arrangement for a strippy quilt is to position the blocks and strips in vertical rows. However, horizontal rows can also create a strippy quilt. These spools are the perfect block for the sewing theme fabric used in the horizontal strips and borders.

Strippy Settings

Strippy quilts have been part of the quilting tradition as far back as can be remembered. Early Welsh, English and French quilts were often made by stitching long pieces of fabric together until the quilt top was wide enough to cover a bed. Eventually patchwork in vertical rows alternated with the long fabric strips and the strippy quilt was established as a popular quilt setting.

Spinning Spools

Most strippy quilts have rows of blocks placed in a vertical position. A less common, but equally effective, strippy design places the blocks in horizontal rows. This type of strippy setting is often referred to as a row quilt. Alternating rows of blocks with a feature fabric emphasize the strong horizontal feature of the overall quilt design.

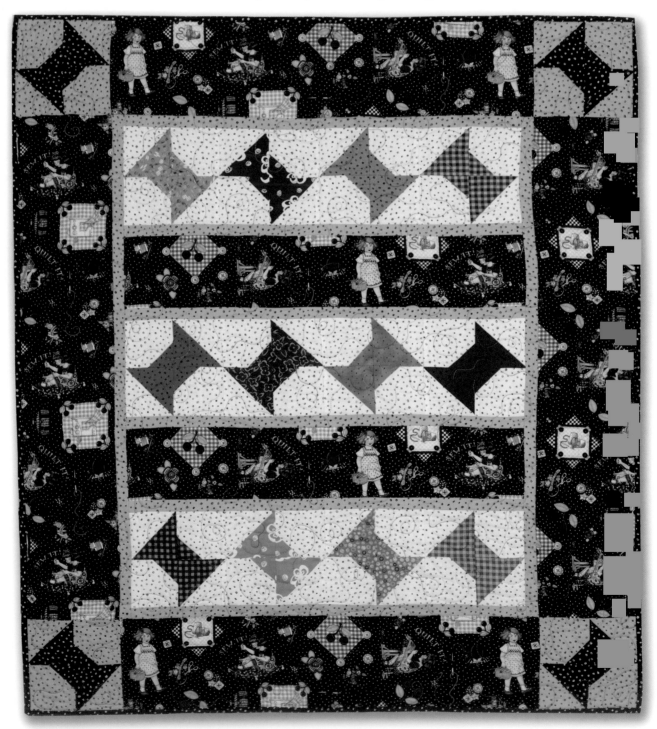

Quilt designed and made by Jean Ann Wright.

Materials

Finished size approximately 37-1/2" x 44-1/2"

Spool blocks: 6" x 6"

wof indicates width of fabric

Note: Sew all blocks with a scant 1/4" seam and press all seams as you sew.

- Fabric A—1 yard sewing theme print (strip rows, borders)

- Fabric B—1/2 yard gold with black dots (sashings, Spool cornerstone blocks)

- Fabric C—1/2 yard black with white dots (Spool cornerstone blocks, binding)

- Fabric D—1/2 yard white with black dots (Spool blocks)

- Fabric scraps—(12) brightly colored prints (Spool blocks)

- Backing—1-1/8 yards

- Thread for machine quilting

- Crib or craft size batting

Note: Sulky® 30 wt Blendables® #4119 Piano Keys thread and Quilter's Dream® Cotton batting were used in this project.

Cutting Instructions

Fabric A, cut:
(2) 6-1/2" x 33" length of fabric border strips.

(2) 6-1/2" x 26" wof strips.

(2) 5" x 24-1/2" wof strips.

Fabric B, cut:
(1) 3-1/2" x wof strip, from this strip cut:
   (8) 3-1/2" squares.

(1) 3-7/8" x wof strip, from this strip cut:
   (4) 3-7/8" squares.

(6) 1-1/4" x wof strips, sew together end-to-end and cut:
   (6) 1-1/4" x 24-1/2" sashing strips and
   (2) 1-1/4" x 33" sashing strips.

Fabric C, cut:
(1) 3-7/8" x wof strip, from this strip cut:
   (4) 3-7/8" squares.
   Trim the remainder of the strip to 2", from this strip cut:
   (8) 2" squares.

(4) 2-1/4" x wof strips, sew together end-to-end for binding.

Fabric D, cut:
(2) 3-1/2" x wof strips, from these strips cut:
   (24) 3-1/2" squares.

(2) 3-7/8" x wof strips, from these strips cut:
   (12) 3-7/8" squares.

Fabric scraps, cut:
(1) 3-7/8" square and
   (2) 2" squares from each of the (12) prints.

Block Assembly

Note: Refer to Half-square Triangle directions on page 9 to construct the Spool blocks.

Spool blocks:
1. Draw a diagonal line from corner to corner on the wrong side of the (12) fabric D 3-7/8" squares.

D

103

2. Lay a marked fabric D 3-7/8" square on a bright print 3-7/8" square, right sides together. Stitch 1/4" on each side of the drawn line. Cut on the drawn line and press toward the bright print triangle to make (2) half-square triangle units.

3. Use the remaining fabric D 3-7/8" squares and bright print 3-7/8" squares to make (2) half-square triangle units in each color for a total of (24) half-square triangle units.

4. Lay a bright color 2" square in one corner of a fabric D 3-1/2" square, right sides together. Sew in a diagonal line across the 2" square and through the fabric layers as shown. Trim 1/4" away from the sewn line and press seams toward the triangle. Use the remaining bright print 2" squares and fabric D 3-1/2" squares to make (2) in each color for a total of (24).

Make 24

5. Lay out (2) matching half-square triangle units and (2) matching units from step 5 as shown. Sew the units together to make a Spool block. Make (12) Spool blocks.

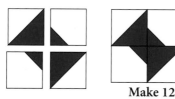

Make 12

Spool cornerstone blocks:

Following the Spool block instructions, make (4) Spool cornerstone blocks using the fabric B and C 3-7/8" squares, the fabric B 3-1/2" squares and the fabric C 2" squares.

Make 4

Row Assembly

1. Referring to the Quilt Assembly Diagram for placement, lay out the Spool blocks in (3) rows with (4) blocks in each row. Sew the blocks together to make (3) Spool block rows.

2. Sew a fabric B 1-1/4" x 24-1/2" sashing strip to each side of a fabric A 5" x 24-1/2" strip to make a strip row. Make (2) strip rows.

Make 2

Quilt Center Assembly

1. Referring to the Quilt Assembly Diagram, lay out the (3) block rows and the (2) strip rows. Sew the rows together to complete the quilt center.

2. Sew the remaining fabric B 1-1/4" x 24-1/2" sashing strips to the top/bottom of the quilt center. Press seams toward the sashing strips. Sew the fabric B 1-1/4" x 33" sashing strips to opposite sides of the quilt center and press toward the sashing strips.

Borders

1. Referring to the Quilt Assembly Diagram, sew the fabric A 6-1/2" x 33" border strips to opposite sides of the quilt center. Press seams toward the border strips.

2. Referring to the Quilt Assembly Diagram for spool orientation, sew a Spool cornerstone block to each end of the fabric A 6-1/2" x 26" border strips. Sew the pieced border strips to the top/bottom of the quilt center.

Finishing the Quilt

Layer the backing fabric, batting and quilt top. Baste the layers together. Hand or machine quilt as desired. Bind to finish the quilt.

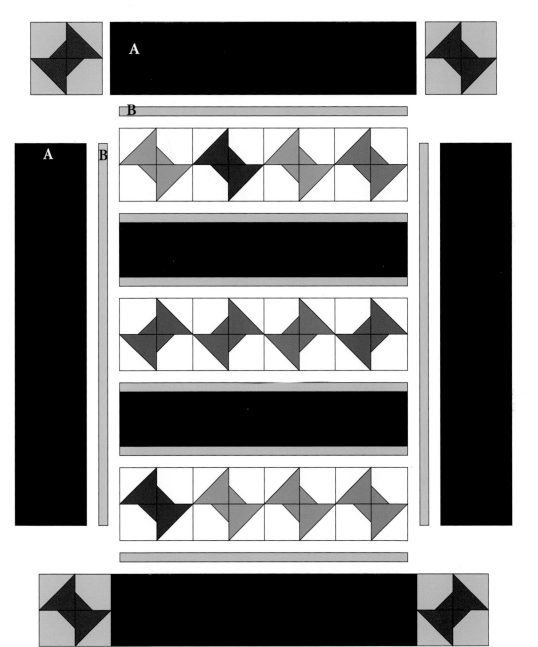

Quilt Assembly Diagram

Isle of Palms

The rows in a strip set quilt do not always need to be the same width. The center of the Isle of Palms quilt features a large print fabric, Flying Geese units, and Garden Mosaic blocks in vertical strips of varying widths. Don't be afraid to mix things up.

Quilt designed and made by Jean Ann Wright.

Materials

Finished size approximately: 60" x 78"

Garden Mosaic blocks: 12-1/2" x 12-1/2"

Flying Geese blocks: 3" x 6"

wof indicates width of fabric

Note: Sew all blocks with a scant 1/4" seam and press all seams as you sew.

- Fabric A—2 yards large scale tropical or floral print (Garden Mosaic blocks, strip rows)
- Fabric B—1-3/4 yards light green foliage print (outer borders)
- Fabric C—1-1/2 yards light mint geometric lattice print (outer borders)
- Fabric D—3/4 yard hunter green swirl print (Garden Mosaic blocks, pieced border rows)
- Fabric E—1 yard medium olive green small leaf print (Garden Mosaic blocks, Flying Geese blocks, inner borders)
- Fabric F—1/2 yard medium mint green print (Garden Mosaic blocks)
- Fabric G—3/4 yard small scale light green check print (pieced border rows, binding)
- Fabric H—1/2 yard bright lime green (Flying Geese blocks)
- Fabric I—1/4 yard light gray/green mini-dot (pieced border rows)
- Backing—4-1/4 yards
- Thread for machine quilting
- Queen size batting

Note: Sulky® 30 wt Blendables® #4017 Lime Sherbet thread and Quilter's Dream® Orient batting were used in this project.

Cutting Instructions

Fabric A, fussy cut:
(2) 10-1/2" x 60-1/2" length of fabric strips, centering the motif in the strips.

(1) 6-3/16" x wof strip, from this strip cut:
(5) 6-3/16" squares.

Fabric B, fussy cut:
(2) 7" x 60-1/2" length of fabric strips, centering the motif in the strips.

Fabric C, fussy cut:
(4) 8-1/2" x wof strips, cutting so the top and bottom of the strips can be matched when sewn together. Sew strips together end to end and cut:
(2) 8-1/2" x 60-1/2" outer border strips.
Note: The size of the strips may vary as you match the fabric pattern, so be flexible with the measurement.

Fabric D, cut:
(2) 4-7/8" x wof strips, from these strips cut:
(10) 4-7/8" squares; cut each square in half on the diagonal once to make (20) 4-7/8" half-square triangles.

(3) 1-1/2" x wof strips, sew together end-to-end and cut:
(2) 1-1/2" x 60-1/2" strips.

Fabric E, cut:
(4) 3-1/2" x wof strips, from these strips cut:
(20) 3-1/2" x 6-1/2" rectangles.

(4) 1-1/2" x wof strips, sew together end-to-end and cut:
(2) 1-1/2" x 60-1/2" top/bottom inner border strips.

(1) 5-1/4" x wof strip, from this strip cut:
(5) 5-1/4" squares; cut each square in half on the diagonal twice to make (20) quarter-square triangles.

Fabric F, cut:
(3) 3-3/8" x wof strips, from these strips cut:
(20) 3-3/8" x 6-3/16" rectangles.

Fabric G, cut:
(3) 2-1/2" x wof strips, sew together end-to-end and cut:
(2) 2-1/2" x 60-1/2" strips.

(7) 2-1/4" x wof strips, sew together end-to-end for binding.

Fabric H, cut:
(4) 3-1/2" x wof strips, from these strips cut:
(40) 3-1/2" squares.

Fabric I, cut:
(3) 1-1/2" x wof strips, sew together end-to-end and cut:
(2) 2-1/2" x 60-1/2" strips.

Block Assembly

Note: Refer to Flying Geese block directions on page 12 to construct the block.

Garden Mosaic blocks:

1. Sew a fabric D 4-7/8" half-square triangle to one side of a fabric F 3-3/8" x 6-3/16" rectangle to make a D/F unit. Make (20) D/F units.

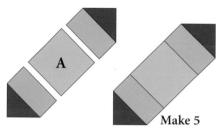

Make 20

2. Sew (2) D/F units to opposite sides of a fabric A 6-3/16" square to make a center unit. Make (5) center units.

Make 5

3. Sew a fabric E 5-1/4" quarter-square triangle to each side of the remaining D/F units to make a side unit. Make (10) side units.

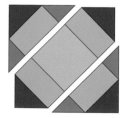

Make 10

4. Lay out (2) side units and (1) center unit. Sew the units together to make a Garden Mosaic block. Make (5) Garden Mosaic blocks.

Make 5

Flying Geese blocks:

1. Lay a fabric H 3-1/2" square on one end of a fabric E 3-1/2" x 6-1/2" rectangle, right sides together. Sew from corner to corner in a diagonal line.

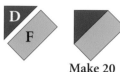

2. Trim 1/4" away from the stitched line and press the seam toward the triangle. Repeat on the opposite side of the rectangle to make a Flying Geese block. Make (20) Flying Geese blocks.

Make 20

Row Assembly

1. Referring to the Quilt Assembly Diagram, sew the (5) Garden Mosaic blocks together in a vertical row. Press seams in one direction to make a center row.

2. Sew (10) Flying Geese blocks together end-to-end in a vertical row. Make (2) Flying Geese rows. Referring to the Quilt Assembly Diagram, sew a fabric D 1-1/2" x 60-1/2" strip to the outside of each Flying Geese row.

3. Sew a fabric G 2-1/2" x 60-1/2" strip and a fabric I 2-1/2" x 60-1/2" strip together to make a G/I row. Make (2) G/I rows.

4. Referring to the Quilt Assembly Diagram, sew a G/I row to the Flying Geese row to make a pieced border row. Make (2) pieced border rows.

Quilt Center Assembly

Referring to the Quilt Assembly Diagram, lay out (2) fabric A 10-1/2" x 60-1/2" strips, the center row and (2) pieced border rows. Sew the rows together to make the quilt center.

Borders

1. Referring to the Quilt Assembly Diagram, sew the fabric B 7" x 60-1/2" strips to opposite sides of the quilt center.

2. Sew a fabric E 1-1/2" x 60-1/2" inner border strip to the fabric C 8-1/2" x 60-1/2" outer border strip to make a top/bottom border. Make (2) top/bottom borders. Sew the top/bottom borders to the top/bottom of the quilt center to complete the quilt.

Finishing the Quilt

Layer the backing fabric, batting and quilt top. Baste the layers together. Hand or machine quilt as desired. Bind to finish the quilt.

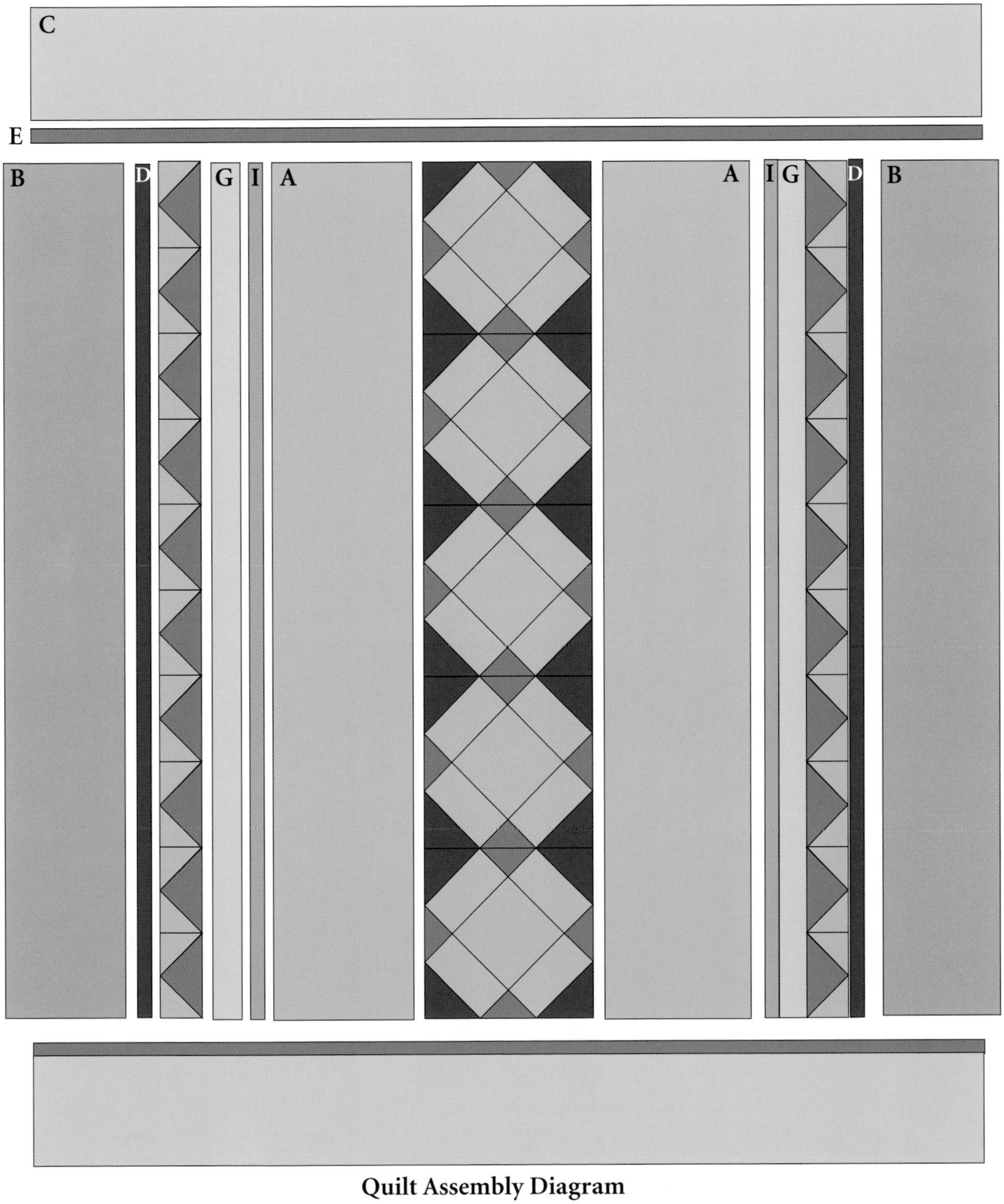

C

E

B　D　G I A　　　　A I G　D B

Quilt Assembly Diagram

Streak of Lightning

Traditional strippy quilts, like this Streak of Lightning, fit into the modern quilting world with ease. It is a great setting choice for a scrap quilt or a coordinated fabric collection. It uses two focus fabrics, one for the vertical sashings and another for the outside borders.

Quilt designed by Jean Ann Wright.

Materials

Finished size approximately 67" x 89"

Flying Geese blocks: 4" x 8"

wof indicates width of fabric

Note: Sew all blocks with a scant 1/4" seam and
press all seams as you sew.

- Fabric A—2-1/4 yards large scale floral print
  (outer borders)

- Fabric B—2-1/8 yards paisley stripe (strip rows)

- Fabric C—2-1/4 yards pale gold texture print
  (Flying Geese blocks)

- Fabric D–1 yard dark gold texture print
  (inner borders, binding)

- Fabric E—1/3 yard orange print
  (Flying Geese blocks)

- Fabric F—1/3 yard rust-orange print
  (Flying Geese blocks)

- Fabric G—1/3 yard olive green print
  (Flying Geese blocks)

- Fabric H—1/3 yard dark olive texture print
  (Flying Geese blocks)

- Fabric I—1/2 yard brown allover mini-flower print
  (Flying Geese blocks)

- Fabric J—1/3 yard red allover flower print
  (Flying Geese blocks)

- Fabric K—1/3 yard dark red texture print
  (Flying Geese blocks)

- Fabric L—1/3 yard bright yellow/gold print
  (Flying Geese blocks)

- Backing—5-1/4 yards

- Thread for machine quilting

- Queen size batting

Note: Sulky® 30 wt Blendables® #4006 Autumn
thread and Quilter's Dream Orient® batting
were used in this project.

Cutting Instructions

Fabric A, cut:
(8) 7-1/2" x wof strips, centering on same floral motif
in each strip, and sew together end to end.
From the sewn strip cut:
(2) 7-1/2" x 75-1/2" side outer border strips and
(2) 7-1/2" x 67-1/2" top/bottom outer border strips.

Fabric B, fussy cut:
(3) 6-1/2" x 72-1/2" length of fabric strips, centering
the motif in the strips.

Fabric C, cut:
(16) 4-1/2" x wof strips, from these strips cut:
(136) 4-1/2" squares.

(1) 4-7/8" x wof strip, from this strip cut:
(4) 4-7/8" squares.

Fabric D, cut:
(7) 2" x wof strips, sew together end-to-end and cut:
(2) 2" x 72-1/2" side inner border strips and
(2) 2" x 53-1/2" top/bottom inner border strips.

(9) 2-1/4" x wof strips, sew together end-to-end for binding.

Fabric E, cut:
(1) 4-7/8" x wof strip, from this strip cut:
(1) 4-7/8" square; cut the square in half on the diagonal
once to make (2) half-square triangles.

Trim the remainder of the 4-7/8" strip to 4-1/2",
from this strip cut:
(4) 4-1/2" x 8-1/2" rectangles.

(1) 4-1/2" x wof strip, from this strip cut:
(4) 4-1/2" x 8-1/2" rectangles.

Fabric F, cut:
(1) 4-7/8" x wof strip, from this strip cut:
(1) 4-7/8" square; cut the square in half on the diagonal
once to make (2) half-square triangles.

Trim the remainder of the 4-7/8" strip to 4-1/2",
from this strip cut:
(4) 4-1/2" x 8-1/2" rectangles.

(1) 4-1/2" x wof strip, from this strip cut:
(4) 4-1/2" x 8-1/2" rectangles.

Fabric G, cut:
(1) 4-7/8" x wof strip, from this strip cut:
(1) 4-7/8" square; cut the square in half on the diagonal
once to make (2) half-square triangles.

Trim the remainder of the 4-7/8" strip to 4-1/2",
from this strip cut:
(4) 4-1/2" x 8-1/2" rectangles.

(1) 4-1/2" x wof strip, from this strip cut:
(4) 4-1/2" x 8-1/2" rectangles.

Fabric H, cut:
(2) 4-1/2" x wof strips, from these strips cut:
    (8) 4-1/2" x 8-1/2" rectangles.

Fabric I, cut:
(3) 4-1/2" x wof strips, from these strips cut:
    (12) 4-1/2" x 8-1/2" rectangles.

Fabric J, cut:
(2) 4-1/2" x wof strips, from these strips cut:
    (8) 4-1/2" x 8-1/2" rectangles.

Fabric K, cut:
(2) 4-1/2" x wof strips, from these strips cut:
    (8) 4-1/2" x 8-1/2" rectangles.

Fabric L, cut:
(1) 4-7/8" x wof strip, from this strip cut:
    (1) 4-7/8" square; cut the square in half on the diagonal once to make (2) half-square triangles. Trim the remainder of the 4-7/8" strip to 4-1/2", from this strip cut:
    (4) 4-1/2" x 8-1/2" rectangles.

(1) 4-1/2" x wof strip, from this strip cut:
    (4) 4-1/2" x 8-1/2" rectangles.

Block Assembly

Note: Refer to the Half-square Triangle and Flying Geese directions on pages 9 and 12 to make the blocks.

Flying Geese blocks:

1. Lay a fabric C 4-1/2" square on a fabric E 4-1/2" x 8-1/2" rectangle, right sides together, as shown. Stitch in a diagonal line across the fabric C 4-1/2" square and through the fabric layers.

2. Trim 1/4" from the sewn line and press the seams toward the triangle.

3. Lay a fabric C 4-1/2" square on the opposite side of the fabric E 4-1/2" x 8-1/2" rectangle. Sew in a diagonal line across the fabric C 4-1/2" square and press the seams toward the triangle to make a C/E Flying Geese block. Make (8) C/E Flying Geese blocks.

Make 8

4. Repeat steps 1 - 3 using the remaining fabric C 4-1/2" squares and the fabric F - L 4-1/2" x 8-1/2" rectangles. Make (8) Flying Geese blocks in the C/F, C/G, C/H, C/J, C/K and C/L color combinations. Make (12) Flying Geese blocks in the C/I color combination for a total of (68) Flying Geese blocks.

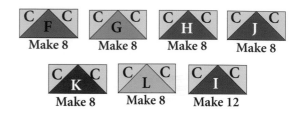

Make 8   Make 8   Make 8   Make 8

Make 8   Make 8   Make 12

Half-square Triangles:

1. Draw a diagonal line from corner to corner on the wrong side of the (4) fabric C 4-7/8" squares.

2. Lay a marked fabric C 4-7/8" square on a fabric E 4-7/8" square, right sides together. Stitch 1/4" on each side of the drawn line. Cut on the drawn line and press toward the darker triangle to make (2) half-square triangle units.

3. Repeat steps 1 - 2 using the remaining fabric C 4-7/8" squares and the fabric F, G and L 4-7/8" squares. Make (2) half-square triangle units in each color combination for a total of (8) half-square triangle units.

Make 2 of each

112

Row Assembly

1. Referring to the Row A Assembly Diagram, lay out (9) Flying Geese blocks and sew together as shown to make row A. Make (4) row A.

2. Referring to the Row B Assembly Diagram and the Quilt Assembly Diagram, lay out (8) Flying Geese blocks and (2) half-square triangle units as shown. Sew the pieces together to make row B. Make (4) row B.

3. Referring to the Streak of Lightning Row Assembly Diagram, sew row A and B together with the long sides of Flying Geese blocks facing to make a streak of lightning row. Make (4) streak of lightning rows.

Quilt Assembly

Referring to the Quilt Assembly Diagram, lay out the (4) streak of lightning rows and the (3) fabric B 6-1/2" x 72-1/2" strip rows to complete the quilt center. Sew the rows together to complete the quilt center.

Borders

1. Referring to the Quilt Assembly Diagram, sew the fabric D 2" x 72-1/2" side inner border strips to opposite sides of the quilt center.

2. Sew the fabric D 2" x 53-1/2" top/bottom inner border strips to the top/bottom of the quilt center.

3. Referring to the Quilt Assembly Diagram, sew a fabric A 7-1/2" x 75-1/2" outer border strip to opposite sides of the quilt center.

4. Sew a fabric A 7-1/2" x 67-1/2" outer border strip to the top/bottom of the quilt center.

Finishing the Quilt

Layer the backing fabric, batting and quilt top. Baste the layers together. Hand or machine quilt as desired. Bind to finish the quilt.

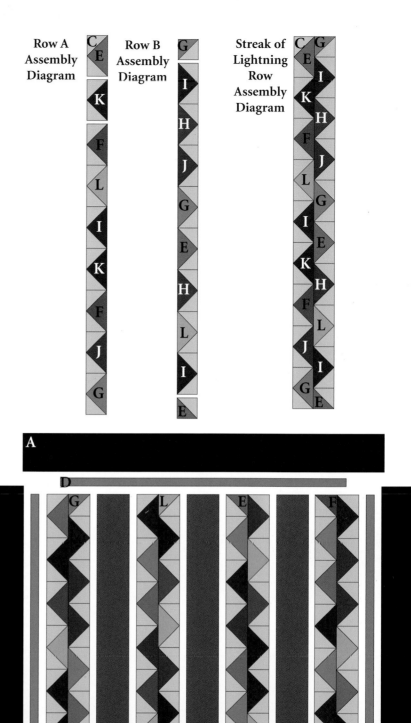

Row A Assembly Diagram

Row B Assembly Diagram

Streak of Lightning Row Assembly Diagram

Quilt Assembly Diagram

113

This Compass Rose medallion quilt was inspired by an antique Welsh design. I combined it with another traditional symbol, the Anglican Compass Rose, to make a unified whole.

Medallion Settings

Medallion quilts are a centuries old quilting tradition. Some of the earliest medallion quilts were the Welsh quilts made many generations ago. These were followed by the Amish quilts and then the patchwork variations that are so popular today. The simplicity of the medallion setting makes this style of quilting quick and easy for today's quilter to design and sew.

Compass Rose

The center block in a medallion quilt is always the most important block in the quilt. This medallion set quilt features a large Mariner's Compass block surrounded by one pieced and two solid borders. To make the Compass Rose or any medallion set quilt larger simply add more borders.

Quilt designed by Jean Ann Wright.

Materials

Finished size approximately 33" x 33"

Compass Rose block: 12" x 12"

wof indicates width of fabric

Note: Sew all blocks with a scant 1/4" seam and press all seams as you sew.

- Fabric A—2/3 yard paisley border in brown, caramel and pink (outer borders)

- Fabric B—1/3 yard rose allover mini-stripe (middle borders)

- Fabric C—1/4 yard brick red (Compass Rose block, pieced borders)

- Fabric D—1/4 yard tan allover floral print (Compass Rose block, pieced borders)

- Fabric E—1/4 yard beige allover print (Compass Rose block, middle borders)

- Fabric F—1/8 yard dark rose print (Compass Rose block, pieced borders)

- Fabric G—1/4 yard pink scattered flowers (pieced borders)

- Fabric H—1/8 yard medium brown allover print (pieced borders)

- Fabric I—1/8 yard gray allover leaf print (Compass Rose block, inner borders)

- Fabric J—1/4 yard black print (Compass Rose block, pieced borders)

- Backing—1-1/8 yards

- Thread for machine quilting

- Craft size batting

- Fabric glue stick

- 10" x 18" piece of stabilizer

Note: Sulky® 30 wt Blendables® #4010 Caramel Apple thread, Quilter's Dream® Cotton batting and Sulky® Soft 'n Sheer Stabilizer were used in this project.

Cutting Instructions

Fabric A, cut:
(4) 4-1/2" x wof strips, from these strips cut:
  (2) 4-1/2" x 25-1/2" side outer border strips and
  (2) 4-1/2" x 33-1/2" top/bottom outer border strips.

Fabric B, cut:
(4) 2-1/2" x wof strips, from these strips cut:
  (4) 2-1/2" x 21-1/2" middle border strips.

Fabric C, cut:
(1) 6-7/8" x wof strip, from this strip cut:
  (2) 6-7/8" squares. From the remainder of the strip cut:
  (1) circle using the template on page 120.
  Trim the remainder of the strip to 4-7/8",
  from this strip cut: (2) 4-7/8" squares.

Fabric D, cut:
(1) 6-7/8" x wof strip, from this strip cut:
  (2) 6-7/8" squares.
  Trim the remainder of the strip to 5-1/4",
  from this strip cut:
  (3) 5-1/4" squares; cut each square in half on the diagonal twice to make (12) quarter-square triangles.

Fabric E, cut:
(1) 5-1/4" square; cut the square in half on the diagonal twice to make (4) quarter-square triangles.
  Use the remainder of the fabric to paper piece the Compass Rose block.

Fabric F, cut:
(4) 2-1/2" squares.
  Use the remainder of the fabric to paper piece the Compass Rose block.

Fabric G, cut:
(1) 4-7/8" x wof strip, from this strip cut:
  (4) 4-7/8" squares; cut the squares in half on the diagonal once to make (8) half-square triangles.

Fabric H, cut:
(1) 3-3/8" x wof strip, from this strip cut:
  (8) 3-3/8" squares.

Fabric I, cut:
(2) 1" x wof strips, from these strips cut:
  (2) 1" x 20-1/2" side inner border strips and
  (2) 1" x 21-1/2" top/bottom inner border strips.
  Use the remainder of the fabric to paper piece the Compass Rose block.

Fabric J, cut:
(1) 4-7/8" x wof strip, from this strip cut:
  (2) 4-7/8" squares. Use the remainder of the fabric to paper piece the Compass Rose block.

Block Assembly

Note: Follow the paper piecing directions on page 119 to make the Compass Rose circle.
Refer to Half-square Triangle directions on page 9 to construct the Pinwheel block.

Half-square Triangles:

1. Draw a diagonal line from corner to corner on the wrong side of the fabric D 6-7/8" squares.

2. Lay a fabric D 6-7/8" square on a fabric C 6-7/8" square, right sides together. Stitch 1/4" on each side of the drawn line. Cut in half on the drawn line and press seams toward darker triangles to make (2) C/D half-square triangle units. Make (4) C/D half-square triangle units.

Make 4

3. Following steps 1 - 2 and using the fabric C and fabric J 4-7/8" squares, make (4) C/J half-square triangle units for inside border corners.

Make 4

Compass Rose block:

1. Sew the (4) paper pieced quarter sections of the compass together to make a circle. Press the joining seams open. Position the compass circle on the stabilizer, right sides together. Stitch around the outside edge of the compass circle on the fabric side. Cut a small slit in the stabilizer, turn right side out and press the seamline sharply.

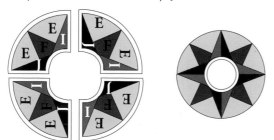

2. Position the fabric C circle on stabilizer, right sides together. Stitch around the outside edge of the circle on the fabric side. Cut a small slit in the stabilizer, turn right side out and press the seamline sharply. Center the fabric C circle on the compass circle, concealing the raw inside edges of the larger compass circle. Stitch in place using your favorite

machine appliqué method. Do not remove the stabilizer on the back of the two circles.

3. Lay out the (4) C/D half-square triangle units as shown. Sew the units together to make a Pinwheel block.

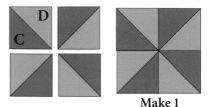
Make 1

4. Center the Compass Rose circle on the Pinwheel block. Appliqué in place. Carefully trim the center of the Pinwheel block away from the back of the Compass Rose circle, trimming approximately 1/4" from the stitching line of the large circle. This will remove excess bulk from the back of the block.

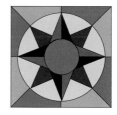

Pieced Borders

1. Referring to the diagram, lay out (2) fabric G 4-7/8" half-square triangles, (3) fabric D 5-1/4" quarter-square triangles, (2) fabric H 3-3/8" squares and (1) fabric E 5-1/4" quarter-square triangle as shown. Sew the pieces together to make a pieced border unit. Make (4) pieced border units.

Make 4

2. Sew a C/J half-square triangle unit to each side of (2) pieced border units as shown. Make (2) pieced top/bottom border units.

Make 2

Quilt Assembly

1. Referring to the Quilt Assembly Diagram on page 121, sew a pieced border unit to opposite sides of the Compass Rose block. Sew the pieced top/bottom border units to the top/bottom of the Compass Rose block to make the quilt center.

2. Referring to the Quilt Assembly Diagram on page 121, sew a fabric I 1" x 20-1/2" side inner border strip to opposite sides of the quilt center. Press toward the border strips. Sew a fabric I 1" x 21-1/2" top/bottom inner border strip to the top/bottom of the quilt center. Press toward the border strips.

3. Sew a fabric B 2-1/2" x 21-1/2" middle border strip to opposite sides of the quilt center. Sew a fabric F 2-1/2" square to each end of the (2) remaining middle border strips. Sew these border strips to the top/bottom of the quilt center.

4. Referring to the Quilt Assembly Diagram on page 121, sew the fabric A 4-1/2" x 25-1/2" side outer border strips to opposite sides of the quilt center. Sew the fabric A 4-1/2" x 33-1/2" top/bottom outer border strips to the top/bottom of the quilt center to complete the quilt top.

Finishing the Quilt

Layer the backing fabric, batting and quilt top. Baste the layers together. Hand or machine quilt as desired. Bind to finish the quilt.

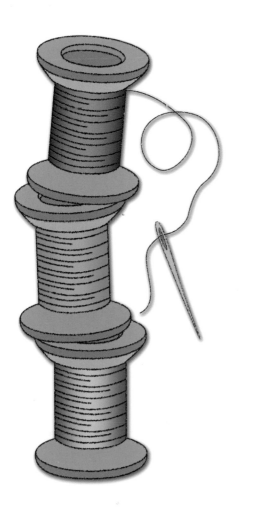

Paper Piecing Method

1. Make (4) copies of the Compass Point template on page 120 for the Compass Rose quarter section, using your choice of paper, such as foundation piecing paper or copy paper.

Make 4

Note: The side of the paper with the pattern lines and numbers is the BACK side of the Fabric BLOCK. The blank side of the paper is the FRONT of the FABRIC BLOCK.

2. Set a narrow machine stitch to help perforate the paper, making it easier to remove.

3. Cut a piece of fabric F large enough to generously cover patch F1 with more than 1/4" all around. Turn the paper pattern over to the BLANK side. Place the F1 fabric right side up on the blank side. Pin or fabric glue to paper.

4. Cut a piece of fabric E large enough to generously cover patch E2 with more than 1/4" all around. Place fabric E2 right side down on top of F1 fabric, pinning in place.

5. Turn the paper over to the printed side. Stitch on the lines between F1 and E2, sewing carefully over pins.

6. Turn the paper over to the blank side. Fold the paper over the just sewn seam line. Printed sides will face each other and the seam allowance of F1 and E2 will extend beyond the fold. Trim seam to 1/4". Unfold paper, open seam allowance, and finger press E2 in place.

7. Repeat steps 3 – 5 to attach, in numerical order, E3, I4 and J5, to the foundation paper. Continue to trim each as in step 5.

8. Trim the outside edges of each quarter section so there is an exact 1/4" seam allowance around the outside edges of each section. The seam allowance is included with your paper pieced pattern so you can carefully cut on the printed line.

9. Remove the paper from the back of the quarter sections. The stitching lines have perforated the paper so it can be torn away. If it is too stubborn to remove, soak it in water for a few minutes and remove the paper. Dry and press by lifting your iron up and down on each section. Do not slide it over the sections as this could stretch the fabric out of shape.

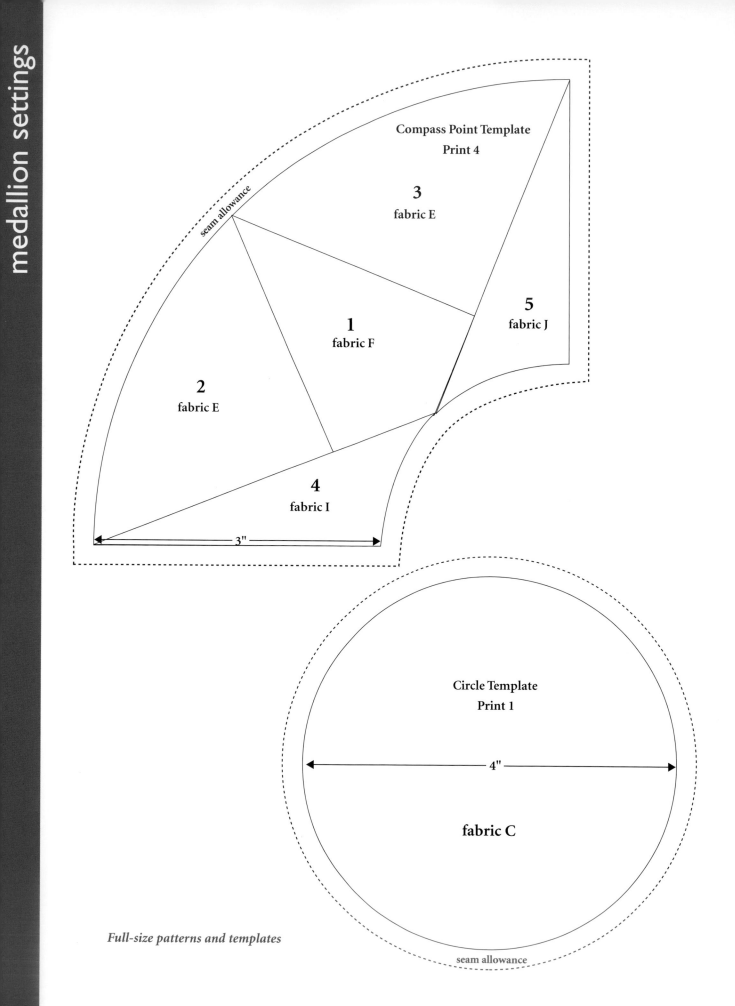

Compass Point Template
Print 4

3

fabric E

5

fabric J

1

fabric F

seam allowance

2

fabric E

4

fabric I

3"

Circle Template
Print 1

4"

fabric C

Full-size patterns and templates

seam allowance

Quilt Assembly Diagram

Kaleidoscope

Medallion set quilts are the perfect way to highlight a favorite focus fabric. Borders in varying
widths and lengths surround the center block and draw attention to the fussy cut
kaleidoscope design element in the center of the quilt.

Quilt designed by Jean Ann Wright.

Materials

Finished size approximately 54" x 66"

Center block: 16" x 16"

Square-in-a-Square blocks: 6" x 6"

wof indicates width of fabric

Note: Sew all blocks with a scant 1/4" seam and press all seams as you sew.

- Fabric A—2/3 yard black with large and small focus designs (Center block, cornerstones)

- Fabric B—1-1/2 yards purple/multi-color large print (border #7)

- Fabric C—1-1/2 yards gold multi-color print (Square-in-a-Square blocks, border #6)

- Fabric D—2/3 yard multi-color wavy print (border #2)

- Fabric E—1/3 yard lavender/mint print (Center block)

- Fabric F—2/3 yard olive print (borders #1 and #3)

- Fabric G—3/4 yard dark purple print (Square-in-a-Square blocks, border #4)

- Fabric H—1/2 yard yellow/gold print (Square-in-a-Square blocks)

- Fabric I—3/4 yard orange print (border #5)

- Backing—3-1/4 yards

- Thread for machine quilting

- Twin size batting

- Stabilizer

Note: Sulky® 30 wt Blendables® #4054 Royal Sampler thread, Quilter's Dream® Cotton batting and Sulky® Soft 'n Sheer Stabilizer were used in this project.

Cutting Instructions

Fabric A, fussy cut:

(1) 11-7/8" x 11-7/8" square.

(4) 4-1/2" squares.

Fabric B, fussy cut:

(3) 8-1/2" x wof strips, sew together end-to-end matching the printed pattern. From the strip cut:
(2) 8-1/2" x 54-1/2" top/bottom border #7 strips.

Fabric C, fussy cut:

(2) 7-1/2" x 48-1/2" border #6 strips on the length of fabric. From the remainder of the fabric fussy cut:
(12) 4" circles, centering identical motifs from the printed fabric in each.

Fabric D, cut:

(4) 3-1/2" x wof strips, from these strips cut:
(4) 3-1/2" x 24-1/2" border #2 strips.
From the remainder of the strips cut:
(8) 3-1/2" squares.

Fabric E, cut:

(1) 9-1/8" x wof strip, from this strip cut:
(2) 9-1/8" squares: cut each square in half on the diagonal once to make (4) half-square triangles.

Fabric F, cut:

(2) 4-1/2" x wof strips, from these strips cut:
(4) 4-1/2" x 16-1/2" border #1 strips.

(3) 3-1/2" x wof strips, sew together end-to-end, from this strip cut:
(4) 3-1/2" x 24-1/2" border #3 strips.
From the remainder of the strip cut:
(4) 3-1/2" squares.

Fabric G, cut:

(5) 1-1/2" x wof strips, from these strips cut:
(2) 1-1/2" x 48-1/2" side border #4 strips and
(2) 1-1/2" x 54-1/2" top/bottom border #4 strips.

(2) 6-1/2" x wof strips, from these strips cut:
(12) 6-1/2" squares.

(1) 3-1/2" x wof strip, from this strip cut:
(4) 3-1/2" squares.

Fabric H, cut:

(4) 3-1/2" x wof strips, from these strips cut:
(48) 3-1/2" squares.

Fabric I, cut:

(5) 1-1/2" x wof strips, sew together end-to-end and cut:
(2) 1-1/2" x 48-1/2" side border #5 strips and
(2) 1-1/2" x 54-1/2" top/bottom border #5 strips.

(7) 2-1/4" x wof strips, sew together end-to-end for binding.

Block Assembly

Note: Refer to Square-in-a-Square blocks directions on page 14 to construct the block.

Square-in-a-Square blocks:

1. Draw a diagonal line from corner to corner on the wrong side of all the fabric H 3-1/2" squares.

2. Lay a fabric H 3-1/2" square on opposite corners of a fabric G 6-1/2" square, right sides together. Stitch on the drawn lines. Trim 1/4" away from the stitching lines and press the triangles open.

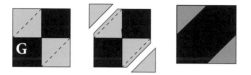

3. Repeat on the remaining two corners of the fabric G 6-1/2" square to make a Square-in-a-Square block. Make (12) Square-in-a-Square blocks.

Make 12

4. Using a compass, draw (12) double circles 3-1/2" and 4" on the stabilizer. Cut out the circles on the 4" line. Lay the stabilizer circles on the right side of the (12) fabric C 4" circles. Stitch the pieces together around the 3-1/2" circle. Cut a 2-1/2" slit through the stabilizer only, turn right side out and press the edges sharply. Make (12) circle appliqués.

5. Center and sew the circle appliqués to the center of the Square-in-a-Square blocks. Make (12) appliqué Square-in-a-Square blocks.

Make 12

Center block:

Sew a fabric E 9-1/8" half-square triangle to opposite sides of the fabric A 11-7/8" square. Press the triangles out. Repeat using the remaining (2) fabric E 9-1/8" half-square triangles to make a center block. Make (1) center block.

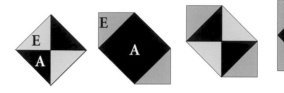

Make 1

Quilt Assembly

Note: Pay close attention to the Quilt Assembly Diagram on page 125 and the quilt photo on page 122 as you add the borders to the center block.

1. Referring to the Quilt Assembly Diagram, sew a fabric F 4-1/2" x 16-1/2" border #1 strip to opposite sides of the center block. Sew a fabric A 4-1/2" square to each side of the remaining fabric F 4-1/2" x 16-1/2" border #1 strips. Sew to the top/bottom of the center block.

2. Sew a fabric D 3-1/2" x 24-1/2" border #2 strip to opposite sides of the bordered center block. Join a fabric G 3-1/2" square to each side of the remaining (2) fabric D 3-1/2" x 24-1/2" border #2 strips. Sew these borders to the top/bottom of the bordered center block.

3. Sew a fabric D 3-1/2" square to each end of the (4) fabric F 3-1/2" x 24-1/2" border #3 strips to make (4) D/F border strips. Sew (2) D/F border strips to opposite sides of the bordered center block. Sew a fabric F 3-1/2" square to each end of the remaining (2) D/F border strips. Sew these borders to the top/bottom of the bordered center block.

4. Sew (6) appliqué Square-in-a-Square blocks together in a row as shown in the Quilt Assembly Diagram. Make (2) Square-in-a-Square rows. Sew the Square-in-a-Square rows to the top/bottom of the bordered center block.

5. Sew a fabric I 1-1/2" x 48-1/2" side border #5 strip and a fabric G 1-1/2" x 48-1/2" side border #4 strip together to make an I/G side border strip. Make (2) I/G side border strips. Sew an I/G side border strip to one side of a fabric C 7-1/2" x 48-1/2" border #6 strip. Repeat with the remaining I/G side border

strip and fabric C border #6 strip. Sew these borders to opposite sides of the bordered center block with fabric G sewn to the other borders.

6. Repeat step 5, sewing the fabric I 1-1/2" x 54-1/2" top/bottom border #5 strips and the fabric G 1-1/2" x 54-1/2" top/bottom border #4 strips together. Sew these border strips to the fabric B 8-1/2" x 54-1/2" top/bottom border #7 strips. Sew these borders to the top/bottom of the bordered center block with fabric G sewn to the other borders.

Finishing the Quilt

Layer the backing fabric, batting and quilt top. Baste the layers together. Hand or machine quilt as desired. Bind to finish the quilt.

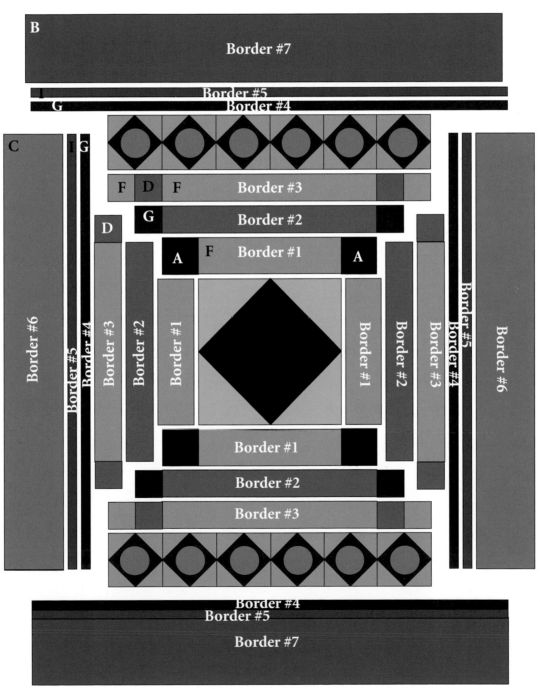

Quilt Assembly Diagram

Spring Basket

Pieced borders alternate with solid border strips and cornerstones to bring attention to the center basket block in this medallion set quilt. A variety of basic pieced blocks make up the individual borders. This pretty quilt looks complicated but is quite simple to sew. Change the quilt's look by using different blocks and fabric colors.

Quilt designed by Jean Ann Wright.

Materials

Finished size approximately 60" x 60"

Basket blocks: 10" x 10"

Thrift blocks: 6" x 6"

Hourglass blocks: 4" x 4"

wof indicates width of fabric

Note: Sew all blocks with a scant 1/4" seam and press all seams as you sew.

- Fabric A—3/4 yard yellow texture print (Basket and Thrift blocks, cornerstones)
- Fabric B—1/2 yard rose print (Basket and Hourglass blocks)
- Fabric C—2/3 yard pink print (Basket, Thrift, Flying Geese and Hourglass blocks)
- Fabric D—1-1/2 yards cream texture print (Thrift, Flying Geese and Hourglass blocks)
- Fabric E—1-1/2 yards red texture print (Thrift blocks, border #2, binding)
- Fabric F—1/3 yard green texture print (Thrift blocks)
- Fabric G—1/2 yard blue texture print (Thrift blocks, border #1)
- Fabric H—1/4 yard dark aqua print (Flying Geese and Hourglass blocks)
- Fabric I—1/2 yard dark green print (Flying Geese blocks, border #3)
- Fabric J—1/3 yard light aqua print (Thrift, Flying Geese and Hourglass blocks)
- Fabric K—1/4 yard brown print (Flying Geese and Hourglass blocks)
- Fabric L—1/3 yard bright gold print (Thrift, Flying Geese and Hourglass blocks)
- Fabric M—1/3 yard medium green print (Thrift, Flying Geese and Hourglass blocks)
- Fabric N—1/3 yard gold print (Flying Geese and Hourglass blocks)
- Backing—4 yards
- Thread for machine quilting
- Queen size batting

Note: Sulky® 30 wt Blendables® #4101 Easter Eggs thread and Quilter's Dream® Orient batting were used in this project.

Cutting Instructions

Fabric A, cut:

(1) 8-7/8" x wof strip, from this strip cut:
   (2) 8-7/8" squares; cut each square in half on the diagonal once to make (4) half-square triangles.
   Trim the remainder of the strip to 4-7/8", from this strip cut:
   (2) 4-7/8" squares; cut each square in half on the diagonal to make (4) half-square triangles.

(3) 2-1/2" x wof strips, from these strips cut:
   (8) 2-1/2" x 6-1/2" strips and (8) 2-1/2" squares.

(2) 4-7/8" x wof strips, from these strips cut:
   (16) 4-7/8" squares; cut each square in half on the diagonal once to make (32) half-square triangles.

Fabric B, cut:

(1) 5-1/4" x wof strip, from this strip cut:
   (4) 5-1/4" squares.
   Trim the remainder of the strip to 4-7/8", from this strip cut:
   (2) 4-7/8" squares; cut each square in half on the diagonal once to make (4) half-square triangles.

(2) 2-7/8" x wof strips, from these strips cut:
   (16) 2-7/8" squares; cut each square in half on the diagonal once to make (32) half-square triangles.

(4) basket handles using the template on page 131.

Fabric C, cut:

(2) 2-7/8" x wof strips, from these strips cut:
   (8) 2-7/8" squares; cut each square in half on the diagonal once to make (16) half-square triangles.
   Trim the remainder of the strip to 2-1/2", from this strip cut:
   (4) 2-1/2" squares.

(1) 3-1/2" x wof strip, from this strip cut:
   (8) 3-1/2" squares.

(1) 5-1/4" x wof strip, from this strip cut:
   (4) 5-1/4" squares.
   Trim the remainder of the strip to 4-1/2", from this strip cut:
   (8) 2-1/2" x 4-1/2" rectangles.

Fabric D, cut:

(4) 4-1/4" x wof strips, from these strips cut:
   (28) 4-1/4" squares; cut each square in half on the diagonal twice to make (112) quarter-square triangles.

(7) 2-1/2" x wof strips, from these strips cut:
   (112) 2-1/2" squares.

(3) 5-1/4" x wof strips, from these strips cut:
   (27) 5-1/4" squares.

Fabric E, cut:

(4) 2-1/2" x wof strips, from these strips cut:
(4) 2-1/2" x 32-1/2" border #2 strips.

(1) 4-7/8" x wof strip, from this strip cut:
(8) 4-7/8" squares; cut each square in half on the diagonal once to make (16) half-square triangles.

(7) 2-1/4" x wof strips, sew together end-to-end for binding.

Fabric F, cut:

(2) 4-7/8" x wof strips, from these strips cut:
(16) 4-7/8" squares; cut each square in half on the diagonal once to make (32) half-square triangles.

Fabric G, cut:

(2) 4-7/8" x wof strips, from these strips cut:
(16) 4-7/8" squares; cut each square in half on the diagonal once to make (32) half-square triangles.

(2) 2-1/2" x wof strips, from these strips cut:
(4) 2-1/2" x 20-1/2" border #1 strips.

Fabric H, cut:

(1) 5-1/4" x wof strip, from this strip cut:
(2) 5-1/4" squares.
Trim the remainder of the strip to 4-1/2",
from this strip cut:
(4) 2-1/2" x 4-1/2" rectangles.

Fabric I, cut:

(6) 2-1/2" x wof strips, sew together end-to-end and cut:
(2) 2-1/2" x 48-1/2" side border #3 strips and
(2) 2-1/2" x 52-1/2" top/bottom border #3 strips.
From the remainder of the strip, cut:
(4) 2-1/2" x 4-1/2" rectangles.

Fabric J, cut:

(1) 5-1/4" x wof strip, from this strip cut:
(4) 5-1/4" squares.
Trim the remainder of the strip to 4-1/2",
from this strip cut:
(8) 2-1/2" x 4-1/2" rectangles.

(1) 3-1/2" x wof strip, from this strip cut:
(4) 3-1/2" squares.

Fabric K, cut:

(1) 5-1/4" x wof strip, from this strip cut:
(4) 5-1/4" squares.
Trim the remainder of the strip to 4-1/2",
from this strip cut:
(8) 2-1/2" x 4-1/2" rectangles.

Fabric L, cut:

(1) 5-1/4" x wof strip, from this strip cut:
(4) 5-1/4" squares.
Trim the remainder of the strip to 4-1/2",
from this strip cut:
(8) 2-1/2" x 4-1/2" rectangles.

(1) 3-1/2" x wof strip, from this strip cut:
(8) 3-1/2" squares.

Fabric M, cut:

(1) 5-1/4" x wof strip, from this strip cut:
(4) 5-1/4" squares.
Trim the remainder of the strip to 4-1/2",
from this strip cut:
(8) 2-1/2" x 4-1/2" rectangles.

(1) 3-1/2" x wof strip, from this strip cut:
(8) 3-1/2" squares.

Fabric N, cut:

(1) 5-1/4" x wof strip, from this strip cut:
(4) 5-1/4" squares.
Trim the remainder of the strip to 4-1/2",
from this strip cut:
(8) 2-1/2" x 4-1/2" rectangles.

Block Assembly

Note: Refer to Quarter-square Triangle, Flying Geese and Thrift block directions on pages 10, 12 and 20 to construct the blocks.

Basket blocks:

1. Appliqué a basket handle to a fabric A 8-7/8" half-square triangle using your favorite appliqué method. Make (4) basket handle triangles.

Make 4

2. Lay a fabric B 2-7/8" half-square triangle on a fabric C 2-7/8" half-square triangle, right sides together. Sew the pieces together along the long edge of the triangles. Press open to make a B/C half-square triangle block. Make (16) B/C half-square triangle blocks.

Make 16

3. Sew the B/C half-square triangle blocks together in pairs as shown. Sew a fabric B 2-7/8" half-square triangle to one edge of each half-square triangle pair, watching the orientation of the triangles. Make a total of (8) triangle strip units.

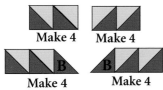

Make 4   Make 4

Make 4   Make 4

4. Sew a triangle strip unit to one side of a fabric B 4-7/8" half-square triangle as shown. Make (4).

Make 4

5. Sew a fabric C 2-1/2" square to the end of (4) triangle strip units as shown. Sew this unit to the edge of the unit made in step 4 to make a basket center unit. Make (4) basket center units.

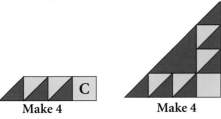

Make 4   Make 4

6. Sew a fabric B 2-7/8" half-square triangle to a fabric A 2-1/2" x 6-1/2" strip watching the orientation of the triangles. Make a total of (8) B/A strips. Sew these units to opposite sides of the basket center units to complete the basket base. Make (4) basket bases.

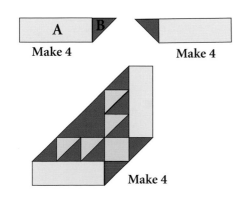

Make 4   Make 4

Make 4

7. Lay out the basket handle triangle, the basket base and a fabric A 4-7/8" half-square triangle as shown. Sew the pieces together to make the Basket block. Make (4) Basket blocks.

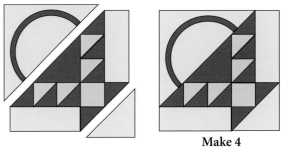

Make 4

8. Referring to the Quilt Assembly Diagram on page 131, sew the (4) Basket blocks together to make the quilt center.

Flying Geese blocks:

1. Lay a fabric D 2-1/2" square on one end of a fabric C 2-1/2" x 4-1/2" rectangle, right sides together. Sew from corner to corner in a diagonal line. Trim 1/4" away from the stitched line and press the seam toward the triangle. Repeat on the opposite side of the rectangle to make a D/C Flying Geese block. Make (8) D/C Flying Geese blocks.

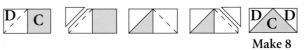

Make 8

2. Repeat step 1 using the remaining fabric D 2-1/2" squares and the fabric H - N 2-1/2" x 4-1/2" rectangles. Make a total of (56) Flying Geese blocks.

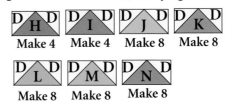

Make 4   Make 4   Make 8   Make 8

Make 8   Make 8   Make 8

Thrift blocks:

1. Lay fabric D 4-1/4" quarter-square triangles on opposite sides of a fabric J 3-1/2" square, right sides together, and sew in place. Press the seams toward the triangles.

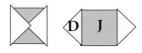

2. Lay fabric D 4-1/4" half-square triangles on the remaining sides of the fabric J 3-1/2" square, right sides together, and sew in place. Press the seams toward the triangles to make a center unit.

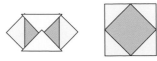

129

3. Lay fabric E 4-7/8" half-square triangles on opposite sides of the center unit, right sides together, and sew in place. Press seams toward the triangles. Lay fabric E 4-7/8" half-square triangles on the remaining sides of the center unit, right sides together, and sew in place. Press the seams toward the triangles to complete a E/D/J Thrift block. Make (4) E/D/J Thrift blocks.

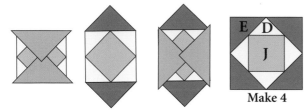

Make 4

4. Repeat steps 1 - 3 using the remaining fabric D 4-1/4" quarter-square triangles, the fabric C, L and M 3-1/2" squares and the fabric A, F and G 4-7/8" half-square triangles. Make a total of (28) Thrift blocks.

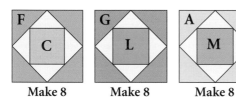

Make 8   Make 8   Make 8

Hourglass blocks:

1. Draw a diagonal line from corner to corner in both directions on the back of the fabric D 5-1/4" squares. Lay a marked fabric D square on a fabric C 5-1/4" square, right sides together. Stitch 1/4" on either side of the drawn line. Cut the squares apart on the drawn line and press seams toward the darker fabric to make (2) half-square triangle units.

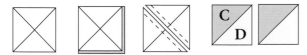

2. Layer the half-square triangle units, right sides together, with the fabric D triangle on the fabric C triangle. Finish drawing the diagonal line on the fabric C triangle. Stitch 1/4" on either side of the drawn line. Cut the squares apart on the drawn line and press seams toward the darker fabric to make (2) Hourglass blocks. Repeat to make (8) D/C Hourglass blocks.

3. Following steps 1 - 2, use the remaining marked fabric D 5-1/4" squares and the fabric B, H and J - N 5-1/4" squares to make a total of (56)

Hourglass blocks.

Make 8   Make 8   Make 8   Make 8   Make 7   Make 5   Make 4

Row Assembly
Flying Geese block rows:

1. Lay out (12) Flying Geese blocks as shown. Sew blocks together to make a Flying Geese block side row. Make (2) Flying Geese block side rows.

Make 2 Flying Geese Side Rows

2. Lay out (14) Flying Geese blocks as shown. Sew blocks together to make a row. Make (2) rows. Sew the remaining Flying Geese units together in pairs. Sew one of the pairs to each of the rows to make a Flying Geese top/bottom block row. Make (2) Flying Geese block top/bottom rows.

Make 1 Flying Geese Top Row and 1 Bottom Row

Thrift block rows:

1. Lay out (6) Thrift blocks as shown in the Quilt Assembly Diagram. Sew blocks together to make a Thrift block side row. Make (2) Thrift block side rows.

2. Lay out (8) Thrift blocks as shown in the Quilt Assembly Diagram. Sew blocks together to make a Thrift block top/bottom row. Make (2) Thrift block top/bottom rows.

Hourglass block rows:

1. Referring to the Quilt Assembly Diagram, lay out (13) Hourglass blocks as shown. Sew the blocks together to make an Hourglass block side row. Make (2) Hourglass block side rows.

2. Lay out (15) Hourglass blocks as shown in the Quilt Assembly Diagram. Sew the blocks together to make an Hourglass block top/bottom row. Make (2) Hourglass block top/bottom rows.

Quilt Assembly

Note: Pay close attention to the Quilt Assembly Diagram and the quilt photo on page 126 as you add the rows and borders to the quilt center.

1. Referring to the Quilt Assembly Diagram, sew a fabric G 2-1/2" x 20-1/2" border #1 strip to opposite sides of the quilt center. Sew a fabric A 2-1/2" square to each end of the remaining fabric

130

G 2-1/2" x 20-1/2" border #1 strips and sew to the top/bottom of the quilt center.

2. Sew the Flying Geese block side rows to the quilt center. Sew the Flying Geese block top/bottom rows to the quilt center.

3. Sew a fabric E 2-1/2" x 32-1/2" border #2 strip to opposite sides of the quilt center. Sew a fabric A 2-1/2" square to each end of the remaining fabric E 2-1/2" x 32-1/2" border #2 strips and sew to the top/bottom of the quilt center.

4. Sew the Thrift block side rows to the quilt center. Sew the Thrift block top/bottom rows to the quilt center.

5. Sew a fabric I 2-1/2" x 48-1/2" side border #3 strip to opposite sides of the quilt center. Sew a fabric I 2-1/2" x 52-1/2" top/bottom border #3 strip to the top/bottom of the quilt center.

6. Sew the Hourglass block side rows to opposite sides of the quilt center. Sew the Hourglass block top/bottom rows to the top/bottom of the quilt center to complete the quilt.

Finishing the Quilt

Layer the backing fabric, batting and quilt top. Baste the layers together. Hand or machine quilt as desired. Bind to finish the quilt.

**Basket Handle Template
Make 4**

Quilt Assembly Diagram

This happy little quilt looks like a complex design, but when it is made one block at a time and put together with spacers, it is a snap to sew.

Circle of Nine Settings

My sister, Janet Houts, and I created the Circle of Nine setting approximately five years ago. We were designing quilts for fabric manufacturers and needed a fresh approach to setting blocks into a quilt. Since then, we have written a book, *Circle of Nine*, to teach quilters how to use this unique setting in a quilt. Since it is a new setting system we felt it should be included in this comprehensive book about sashings and settings.

Tropical Smoothie

Triangles and squares are the most basic quilting shapes. The arrangement of these simple, geometric shapes in a finished quilt can produce a design that is deceptively complex in appearance. The Circle of Nine setting is the perfect way to transform simplicity into sophistication.

Quilt designed by Jean Ann Wright.

Materials

Finished size approximately 40" x 40"

Triangle Square blocks: 8" x 8"

Square-in-a-Square blocks: 4" x 4"

wof indicates width of fabric

Note: Sew all blocks with a scant 1/4" seam and press all seams as you sew.

- Fabric A—1/2 yard aqua print (Triangle Square blocks, outer borders)

- Fabric B—1/2 yard lime green print (Triangle Square blocks, outer borders)

- Fabric C—1 yard yellow/white floral print (Triangle Square blocks and Square-in-a-Square blocks)

- Fabric D—1/3 yard multi-color leaf print (Triangle Square blocks and Square-in-a-Square blocks)

- Fabric E—1/2 yard bright multi-color floral print (Triangle Square blocks and Square-in-a-Square blocks, spacers)

- Fabric F—2/3 yard magenta texture print (inner border, binding)

- Backing—1-1/4 yards

- Thread for machine quilting

- Craft size batting

Note: Sulky® 30 wt Blendables® #4057 Fresh Butter thread and Quilter's Dream® Orient batting were used in this project.

Cutting Instructions

Fabric A, cut:
(2) 3-1/2" x wof strips, from these strips cut:
  (2) 3-1/2" x 17-1/2" side outer border strips and
  (2) 3-1/2" x 20-1/2" top/bottom outer border strips.

(2) 2-7/8" x wof strips, from these strips cut:
  (18) 2-7/8" squares.

Fabric B, cut:
(2) 3-1/2" x wof strips, from these strips cut:
  (2) 3-1/2" x 17-1/2" side outer border strips and
  (2) 3-1/2" x 20-1/2" top/bottom outer border strips.

(2) 2-7/8" x wof strips, from these strips cut:
  (18) 2-7/8" squares.

Fabric C, cut:
(3) 2-7/8" x wof strips, from these strips cut:
  (36) 2-7/8" squares.

(1) 2-1/2" x wof strip, from this strip cut:
  (8) 2-1/2" x 4-1/2" rectangles.

(5) 2-1/2" x wof strips, from these strips cut:
  (68) 2-1/2" squares.

Fabric D, cut:
(1) 4-1/2" x wof strip, from this strip cut:
  (8) 4-1/2" squares.

(2) 2-1/2" x wof strips, from these strips cut:
  (32) 2-1/2" squares.

Fabric E, cut:
(1) 4-1/2" x wof strip, from this strip cut:
  (9) 4-1/2" squares.

(2) 4-1/2" x wof strips, from these strips cut:
  (8) 4-1/2" x 8-1/2" rectangles.

Fabric F, cut:
(4) 1-1/2" x wof strips, from these strips cut:
  (2) 1-1/2" x 32-1/2" side inner border strips and
  (2) 1-1/2" x 34-1/2" top/bottom inner border strips.

(5) 2-1/4" x wof strips, sew together end-to-end for binding.

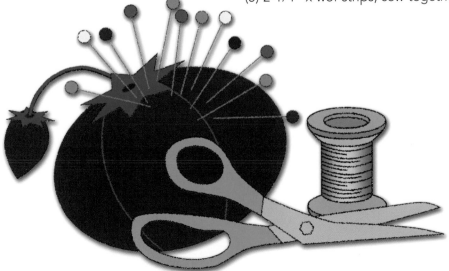

135

Block Assembly

Note: Refer to Half-square Triangle and Square-in-a-Square directions on pages 9 and 14 to construct the blocks.

Square-in-a-Square blocks:

1. Draw a diagonal line from corner to corner on the wrong side of all the fabric C 2-1/2" squares. Lay (2) fabric C squares in opposite corners of a fabric D 4-1/2" square. Stitch on the drawn lines and trim 1/4" from the stitched lines. Press the triangles open.

2. Lay (2) fabric C 2-1/2" squares in the remaining corners of the fabric D 4-1/2" square. Stitch on the drawn lines and trim 1/4" from the stitched lines. Press the triangles open to make a C/D Square-in-a-Square block. Make (8) C/D Square-in-a-Square blocks and (9) C/E Square-in-a-Square blocks for a total of (17) blocks.

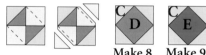

Make 8   Make 9

Half-square Triangle blocks:

1. Draw a diagonal line from corner to corner on the wrong side of all the fabric C 2-7/8" squares. Lay a fabric C 2-7/8" square on a fabric A 2-7/8" square, right sides together. Stitch 1/4" on each side of the drawn line.

2. Cut in half on the drawn line and press seams toward the darker triangle to make (2) A/C half-square triangles. Make (36) A/C half-square triangle blocks.

Make 36

3. Repeat steps 1 - 2 using the remaining fabric C 2-7/8" squares and fabric B 2-7/8" squares. Make (36) B/C half-square triangle blocks.

Make 36

Triangle Square blocks:

1. Sew an A/C half-square triangle block and a B/C half-square triangle block together, as shown, to make a half-square triangle unit. Make (36) half-square triangle units.

Make 36

2. Sew a half-square triangle unit to opposite sides of a C/D Square-in-a-Square block, as shown, to make a C/D center block unit. Make (8) C/D center block units.

Make 8

3. Sew a half-square triangle unit to opposite sides of a C/E Square-in-a-Square block, as shown. Make (1) C/E center block unit.

Make 1

4. Sew a fabric D 2-1/2" square to opposite sides of the remaining half-square triangle units. Make (18).

Make 18

5. Sew these units to the top and bottom of the center block unit to complete a Triangle Square block. Make (8) C/D Triangle Square blocks and (1) C/E Triangle Square block.

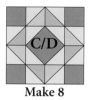

Make 8   Make 1

Spacer Assembly

Sew a fabric C 2-1/2" x 4-1/2" rectangle to opposite sides of a C/E Square-in-a-Square block to make a Spacer unit. Make (4) Spacer units.

Make 4

Quilt Assembly

1. Referring to the Quilt Assembly Diagram, sew a Spacer unit to the top and bottom of the C/E Triangle Squares block. Sew a C/D Triangle Square block to the Spacer units to complete the center vertical row.

2. Referring to the Quilt Assembly Diagram, sew a Spacer unit to one side of (2) C/D Triangle Squares blocks. Sew a fabric E 4-1/2" x 8-1/2" rectangle to one side of the remaining C/D Triangle Square blocks.

3. Sew a C/E Square-in-a-Square block to the remaining fabric E 4-1/2" x 8-1/2" rectangles.

4. Referring to the Quilt Assembly Diagram for placement, sew the units from step 3 to the top or bottom of the remaining C/D Triangle Square blocks. Sew the blocks together as shown in the Quilt Assembly Diagram to complete a side row. Make (2) side rows.

5. Sew the side rows to opposite sides of the center vertical row to complete the quilt center.

Borders

1. Sew the fabric F 1-1/2" x 32-1/2" side inner border strips to opposite sides of the quilt center. Sew the fabric F 1-1/2" x 34-1/2" top/bottom inner border strips to the top/bottom of the quilt center.

2. Sew a fabric A 3-1/2" x 17-1/2" side outer border strip and a fabric B 3-1/2" x 17-1/2" side outer border strip together end-to-end to make an A/B side outer border. Make (2) A/B side outer borders. Sew the A/B side outer borders to opposite sides of the quilt center, referring to the Quilt Assembly Diagram for color placement.

3. Sew a fabric A 3-1/2" x 20-1/2" top/bottom outer border strip and a fabric B 3-1/2" x 20-1/2" top/bottom outer border strip together end-to-end to make an A/B top/bottom outer border. Make (2) A/B top/bottom outer borders. Sew the A/B top/bottom outer borders to the top/bottom of the quilt center, referring to the Quilt Assembly Diagram for color placement.

Finishing the Quilt

Layer the backing fabric, batting and quilt top. Baste the layers together. Hand or machine quilt as desired. Bind to finish the quilt.

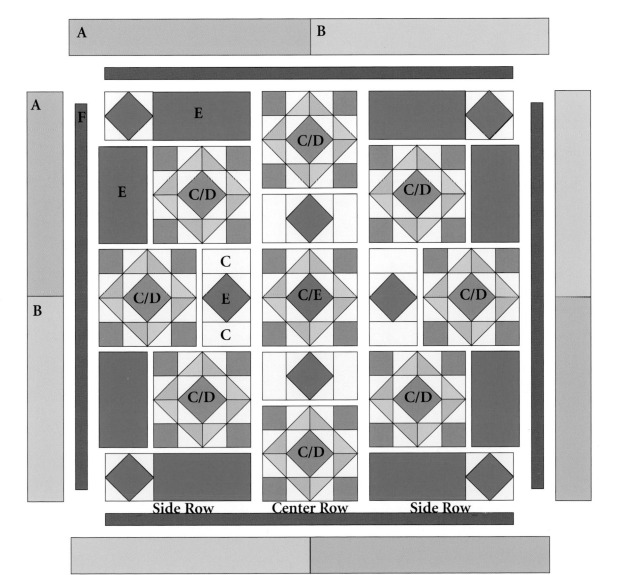

Quilt Assembly Diagram

It's A Puzzlement

King's Crown blocks and Flying Geese spacer units create the overall design in this innovative Circle of Nine quilt setting. Careful placement of the spacer units around the blocks give this quilt the look of interlocking puzzle pieces.

Quilt designed by Janet Houts.

Materials

Finished size approximately 66" x 66"

King's Crown blocks: 12" x 12"

wof indicates width of fabric

Note: Sew all blocks with a scant 1/4" seam and press all seams as you sew.

- Fabric A—2 yards cream texture print (spacers, outer borders)

- Fabric B—1/2 yard olive narrow stripe (inner borders)

- Fabric C—2/3 yard olive woven texture print (spacers)

- Fabric D—3/4 yard gold texture print (King's Crown blocks, spacers, inner borders)

- Fabric E—1/2 yard black floral print (King's Crown blocks)

- Fabric F—1/2 yard black texture print (King's Crown blocks)

- Fabric G—1 yard rust texture print (King's Crown blocks, binding)

- Backing—5 yards

- Thread for machine quilting

- Double size batting

Note: Sulky® 30 wt Blendables® #4010 Caramel Apple thread and Quilter's Dream® Orient batting were used in this project.

Cutting Instructions

Fabric A, cut:

(8) 6-1/2" x wof strips, from these strips cut:
    (4) 6-1/2" x 18 1/2" side outer border strips,
    (4) 6-1/2" x 24-1/2" top/bottom outer border strips and
    (16) 6-1/2" squares.

(3) 3-1/2" x wof strips, from these strips cut:
    (16) 3-1/2" x 6-1/2" rectangles and
    (4) 3-1/2" squares.

Fabric B, cut:

(4) 3-1/2" x wof strips, from these strips cut:
    (8) 3-1/2" x 15-1/2" strips.

Fabric C, cut:

(5) 3-1/2" x wof strips, from these strips cut:
    (56) 3-1/2" squares.

(1) 3-7/8" x wof strip, from this strip cut:
    (8) 3-7/8" squares.

Fabric D, cut:

(2) 3-1/2" x wof strips, from these strips cut:
    (24) 3-1/2" squares.

(1) 3-7/8" x wof strip, from this strip cut:
    (8) 3-7/8" squares.

(2) 4-1/4" x wof strips, from these strips cut:
    (9) 4-1/4" squares; cut each square in half on the diagonal twice to make (36) quarter-square triangles.

Fabric E, cut:

(2) 6-1/2" x wof strips, from these strips cut:
    (9) 6-1/2" squares.

Fabric F, cut:

(3) 4-1/4" x wof strips, from these strips cut:
    (27) 4-1/4" squares; cut each square in half on the diagonal twice to make (108) quarter-square triangles.

Fabric G, cut:

(4) 3-7/8" x wof strips, from these strips cut:
    (36) 3-7/8" squares; cut each square in half on the diagonal once to make (72) half-square triangles.

(7) 2-1/4" x wof strips, sew together end-to-end for binding.

Block Assembly

Note: Refer to Half-square Triangle and Flying Geese block directions on pages 9 and 12 to construct the block.

Half-square Triangles:

1. Draw a diagonal line from corner to corner on the wrong side of all the fabric D 3-7/8" squares.

2. Lay a fabric D 3-7/8" square on a fabric C 3-7/8" square, right sides together. Stitch 1/4" on each side of the drawn line.

3. Cut in half on the drawn line and press seams toward the dark triangle to make (2) C/D half-square triangle units. Make (16) C/D half-square triangle units.

Make 16

Pieced Flying Geese:

I. Lay a fabric D 4-1/4" quarter-square triangle on a fabric F 4-1/4" quarter-square triangle, right sides together. Stitch the triangles together along the long edge and press open. Make (36) D/F squares.

Make 36

2. Sew a fabric F 4-1/4" quarter-square triangle to each side of the D/F squares to make a pieced triangle unit. Make (36) pieced triangle units.

Make 36

3. Sew a fabric G 3-7/8" half-square triangle to each side of the pieced triangle units to make a pieced Flying Geese unit. Make (36) pieced Flying Geese units.

Make 36

King's Crown blocks:

I. Sew a pieced Flying Geese unit to opposite sides of a fabric E 6-1/2" square to make a block center. Make (9) block centers.

Make 9

2. Sew a fabric D 3-1/2" square to each side of a pieced Flying Geese unit. Make (2). Sew these units to the remaining sides of a block center to complete Block A.

Make 2

Make 1
Block A

3. Sew a fabric D 3-1/2" square to one side of a pieced Flying Geese unit as shown.

4. Sew a C/D half-square triangle unit to the opposite side of the pieced Flying Geese unit, carefully watching the orientation of the half-square triangle unit. Make (8) units.

Make 8

5. Sew a step 4 unit to the remaining sides of a block center to complete block B. Make (4) Block B.

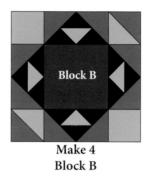
Make 4
Block B

6. Sew a C/D half-square triangle unit to each side of a pieced Flying Geese unit. Make (4) C/D pieced Flying Geese units.

Make 4

7. Sew a fabric D 3-1/2" square to each side of the remaining pieced Flying Geese units Make (4) D pieced Flying Geese units.

Make 4

8. Sew a C/D pieced Flying Geese unit and a D pieced Flying Geese unit to the remaining sides of a block center to complete Block C. Make (4) Block C.

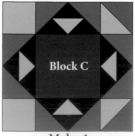
Make 4
Block C

Spacer Unit Assembly

Draw a diagonal line from corner to corner on the back of all the fabric C 3-1/2" squares.

Spacer D units:

1. Lay (2) fabric C 3-1/2" squares in opposite corners of a fabric A 6-1/2" square, right sides together, as shown. Stitch on the drawn lines and trim 1/4" from the sewn lines. Press the triangles open.

2. Lay a fabric C 3-1/2" square on one remaining corner of the fabric A 6-1/2" square, right sides together, as shown. Stitch on the drawn line and trim 1/4" from the sewn line. Press the triangle open. Make (8) units. Sew the units together in pairs as shown to complete a Spacer D unit. Make (4) Spacer D units.

Make 8

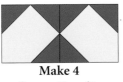

Make 4
Spacer D units

Flying Geese spacer units:

1. Lay a fabric C 3-1/2" square on a fabric A 3-1/2" x 6-1/2" rectangle, right sides together, as shown. Stitch on the drawn line. Trim 1/4" from the sewn line and press the seams toward the triangle.

2. Lay a fabric C 3-1/2" square on the opposite side of the fabric A 3-1/2" x 6-1/2" rectangle. Stitch on the drawn line. Trim 1/4" from the sewn line and press the seams toward the triangle to make a C/A/C Flying Geese spacer unit. Make (8) C/A/C Flying Geese spacer units.

Make 8
Flying Geese
spacer units

Spacer E units:

Lay a fabric C 3-1/2" square on one side of a fabric A 3-1/2" x 6-1/2" rectangle, right sides together, as shown. Stitch on the drawn line. Trim 1/4" from the sewn line and press the seams toward the triangle. Sew a Flying Geese spacer unit to the triangle side of the fabric A 3-1/2" x 6-1/2" rectangle, as shown, to make a Spacer E unit. Make (4) Spacer E units.

Make 4
Spacer E units

Spacer F units:

Lay a fabric C 3-1/2" square on one side of a fabric A 3-1/2" x 6-1/2" rectangle, right sides together, as shown. Stitch on the drawn line. Trim 1/4" from the sewn line and press the seams toward the triangle. Sew a Flying Geese spacer unit to the triangle side of the fabric A 3-1/2" x 6-1/2" rectangle, as shown, to make a Spacer F unit. Make (4) Spacer F units.

Make 4
Spacer F units

Quilt Center Assembly

Block B units:

1. Referring to the Quilt Center Assembly Diagram on page 142, sew a Spacer F unit to the left side of Block B, matching the fabric C triangles.

2. Sew a fabric A 3-1/2" square to the fabric A end of the Spacer E unit. Sew the unit to the top of Block B, matching the fabric C triangles.

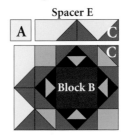
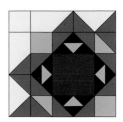

141

3. Referring to the Quilt Center Assembly Diagram, sew a fabric B 3-1/2" x 15-1/2" strip to the left side of Block B, as shown.

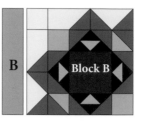

4. Sew a fabric D 3-1/2" square to the left end of a fabric B 3-1/2" x 15-1/2" strip. Sew the B/D strip to the top of block B. Make (4) Block B units.

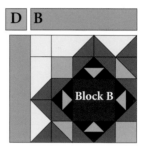

Make 4
Block B units

Block C units:

1. Join a Spacer D unit to Block C, matching the fabric C corner triangles. Make (4) Block C units.

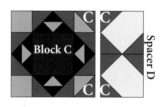

Make 4
Block C units

Quilt Row Assembly

Row 1:

Sew a Block B unit to one side of a Block C unit, carefully following the Quilt Center Assembly Diagram. Sew a Block B unit to the B/C unit, carefully following the Quilt Center Assembly Diagram for orientation of the Block B units.

Block B unit   Block C unit   Block B unit

Row 2:

Referring to the Quilt Center Assembly Diagram, sew a block C unit to one side of Block A, carefully watching the orientation of the Block C unit. Sew a Block C unit to the other side of Block A, carefully watching the orientation of the Block C unit.

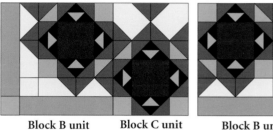

Block C unit   Block A unit   Block C unit

Row 3:

Sew a Block B unit to the one side of a Block C unit, carefully following the Quilt Center Assembly Diagram for orientation of the Block B unit. Sew a Block B unit to the Block B/C unit, carefully watching the Block B orientation.

Block B unit   Block C unit   Block B unit

Sewing the Rows Together

Sew the rows together following the Quilt Center Assembly Diagram to complete the quilt center.

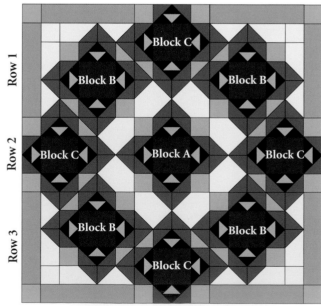

Quilt Center Assembly Diagram

Borders

1. Lay a fabric C 3-1/2" square on one corner of a fabric A 6-1/2" square, right sides together. Sew on the line and trim 1/4" from sewn lines. Press seams toward the triangle to make an A/C unit. Make (8) A/C units.

Make 8

2. Sew the A/C units together in pairs, matching the fabric C triangles. Make (4) pairs.

Make 4

3. Referring to the Quilt Assembly Diagram, sew fabric A 6-1/2" x 18-1/2" side outer border strips to opposite sides of an A/C pair to make a side outer border unit. Make (2) side outer border units. Sew the side outer border units to opposite sides of the quilt center.

Make 2

4. Referring to the Quilt Assembly Diagram, sew fabric A 6-1/2" x 24-1/2" top/bottom outer border strips to opposite sides of an A/C pair to make a top/bottom outer border unit. Make (2) top/bottom outer border units. Sew the top/bottom outer border units to the top/bottom of the quilt center.

Finishing the Quilt

Layer the backing fabric, batting and quilt top. Baste the layers together. Hand or machine quilt as desired. Bind to finish the quilt.

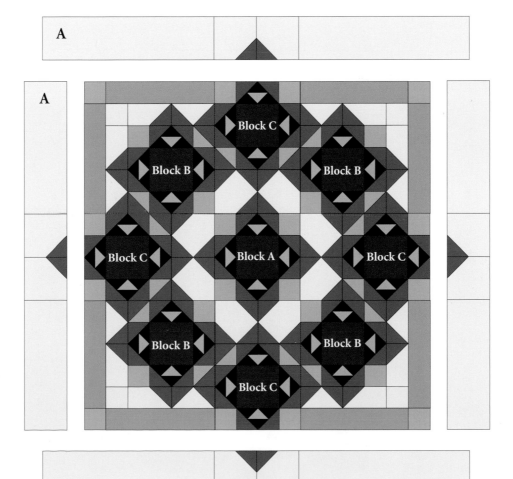

Quilt Assembly Diagram

Shopping Guide

Books

The Elements of Color by Johannes Itten
www.worqx.com/color/itten.htm

Circle of Nine by Janet Houts and Jean Ann Wright
www.landauercorp.com
www.circleofninequilts.com

Materials and Tools

Sulky®
www.sulky.com

Quilter's Dream®
www.QuiltersDreamBatting.com

Creative Grids®
www.creativegridsusa.com

Online Fabric Stores

www.connectingthreads.com

www.equilter.com

www.gloriouscolor.com

www.keepsakequilting.com

www.ladyfingerssewing.com

www.hancocks-paducah.com

Project Fabric Collections

Keep in mind that most fabric collections have a shelf life of about six months. If the exact fabrics aren't available, a trip to your favorite quilt shop or an online fabric store will offer many excellent fabric substitutions to make each of the projects featured in this book.

Asian Allegory
Asian Allegory for Blank Quilting

Piñata Party
Fiesta by Carol Eldridge for Andover Fabrics™

Churn Dash
Kaffe Fassett fabrics by Westminster

Folk Art Posy
Fabrics by Kim Schaefer for Andover Fabrics™

Monkey Business
Anna Griffin fabrics for Windham Fabrics

Compass Rose Quilt
Country Manor by Paula Barnes
for Marcus Fabrics®

Kaleidoscope
Patternista by Paula Nadelstern for Benartex

Spring Basket
Forever Spring by Nancy Halvorsen for Benartex

Tropical Fruit Smoothie
Calypso by Ro Gregg for Fabri-Quilt Paintbrush Studio Collection

It's A Puzzlement
Ginger Rose collection by Nancy Murty for Andover Fabrics™